Writing the
BUSINESS
RESEARCH
PAPER

Writing the
BUSINESS
RESEARCH
PAPER

A Complete Guide

Thomas J. Farrell
Charlotte Donabedian
Johnson & Wales University

CAROLINA ACADEMIC PRESS
DURHAM, NORTH CAROLINA

LCC Number: 91-73930
ISBN: 0-89089-445-0 paper
ISBN: 0-89089-446-9 cloth

Manufactured in the United States of America

Carolina Academic Press
700 Kent Street
Durham, NC 27701
(919) 489-7486

CONTENTS

PREFACE

Writing the Business Research Paper is a text intended for use by undergraduate and graduate students majoring in business subjects. The intent of the book is to provide students with instruction on how to research business topics as well as lessons on how to write and correctly document the business research paper.

The need for such a book is clear. Virtually all existing texts on the writing of research papers have a liberal arts emphasis as far as examples and illustrations used. All references in *Writing the Business Research Paper* have been selected with the interests of business majors in mind. These include lists of suggested business topics (Ch. 2) as well as extensive lists of business indices, journals, and other specialized references that students will find immediately useful (Ch. 3).

The needs of the business major are reflected in other ways in the text. Since business majors are often required to do considerable primary research, time is spent detailing primary techniques such as interviewing and marketing surveys using telephone and mail. Coverage is given to graphics such as tables, charts, and graphs, which are commonly used in business reports to convey statistical information. Also, an important section on the non-sexist use of language is included to prepare the student for the changing modes of communication in an egalitarian society.

The book is organized into ten chapters. Each chapter opens with a set of learning objectives which spells out the specific skills discussed in that chapter. Application Activities conclude eight chapters allowing students to practice their newly acquired skills. Following is a brief description of the contents of each chapter.

Chapter 1—INTRODUCING RESEARCH IN BUSINESS
This chapter provides the student with an understanding of business research and the role research plays in a business career. Two types of papers are discussed.

Chapter 2—PREPARING TO RESEARCH
The second chapter takes students through all of the steps leading up to research from building a research plan to constructing a preliminary outline.

Chapter 3—COLLECTING INFORMATION FOR THE RESEARCH PAPER
This chapter gives students the necessary information to begin collecting information using a wide range of library resources. Lists of specialized business references are included.

Chapter 4—CONDUCTING A DATABASE SEARCH
Students learn how to conduct both online and offline database searches.

Chapter 5—OBTAINING PRIMARY INFORMATION
All of the key primary research techniques from surveys to personal interviews are explained, and a sample survey is presented as an example.

Chapter 6—READING AND TAKING NOTES
This chapter explains the concept of plagiarism and then focuses on efficient note taking techniques.

Chapter 7—WRITING EFFECTIVELY
Basic writing skills needed for writing a successful paper are covered. An extensive section on the use of nonsexist language is offered.

Chapter 8—COMPOSING THE BUSINESS RESEARCH PAPER
Chapter 8 discusses the use of the word processor and other computer technology in writing, and revising a paper. Guidelines for the use of visual aids are included.

Chapter 9—DOCUMENTING BUSINESS SOURCES
The two major styles for documenting sources (MLA and APA) are explained in Chapter 9. The style discussion is followed by complete lists of sample entries for each style.

Chapter 10—FINALIZING THE BUSINESS RESEARCH PAPER
The last chapter explains and illustrates how to assemble the individual parts of the business research paper. Two sample student papers serve as examples of correct documentation in both styles.

The growing number of students who choose to major in business during their post-secondary education will find *Writing the Business Research Paper* a book that meets their needs and interests. That is what it is intended to do, and that is the hope.

We would like to thank our assistants, Wanloe Konyak and Melissa Morin, for their assistance in preparing the manuscript. Thanks also to those who were kind enough to read the manuscript and make suggestions.

Charlotte Donabedian
Thomas J. Farrell

Writing the
BUSINESS RESEARCH PAPER

1
INTRODUCING RESEARCH IN BUSINESS

Learning Objectives

Upon completing this chapter you should be able to:

1. Explain the similarities and differences of medieval academic research and research in today's colleges and universities.
2. Explain how research skills can contribute to the success of an individual or corporate entrepreneur.
3. Explain how an informational research paper differs from an analytical/persuasive research paper.
4. Organize the researcher's journal.
5. Prepare the researcher's work schedule.

INTRODUCING BUSINESS RESEARCH

As a business student about to undertake a business research project, you are continuing a long tradition of scholarly inquiry. The same skills you employ in this project will serve you well in your career, so it is in your self-interest to learn them well. Before you begin, it may be useful to place your activity into its proper historical perspective.

1.1 ACADEMIC RESEARCH: PAST AND PRESENT

Since medieval scholars and students first joined together to form universities during the twelfth century, research has been a primary method of acquiring knowledge. Typically, those early curricula were liberal arts consisting of some combinations of grammar, rhetoric, dialectic, arithmetic, geometry, astronomy, and music. Professors lectured and posed questions, and students spent considerable time in independent research as part of the search for truth. At the end of the term, exams were given and success or failure would depend on the quality of the student's research.

Today, some eight hundred years later, much has changed. Colleges and universities abound, enabling a much greater part of the population to obtain a higher education. Professors lecture to larger groups of students who take notes and are expected to absorb the knowledge being imparted. In too many situations, student roles have become more passive than they once were. Instead of an active quest for knowledge, the idea too often is simply to prove one's ability to recall the material offered in the lecture by passing an exam.

Fortunately, colleges and universities have retained research as a learning tool. Whether it is a research paper at the undergraduate level, a thesis paper for a master's degree, or a challenging dissertation as the last step of a doctoral program, research is still required of today's students. This is much for the good as it is through this active personal involvement in the discovery process that genuine learning occurs.

Modern technology has provided today's student researchers with many advantages not available to the scholar of the Middle Ages. Electronic "online" information services instantly search databases for relevant material. Computers store notes and manuscripts for later retrieval. Word processors allow the student easily to edit copy. However, even with these technological aids, the task of the modern researcher is far more formidable than that of the twelfth century counterpart. The reason is that the body of knowledge has exploded during the twentieth century and continues to grow at an astonishing rate. Estimates are that mankind's knowledge almost doubled during the first half of the twentieth century. It is no longer possible to know all there is to be known, as the early Greek philosophers attempted to do. Instead, in addition to struggling to stay broadly informed, we try to stake out our own specialized area of interest in which we gain some degree of expertise. Research is one of the means by which we acquire such expertise.

Research has also become a major problem-solving tool of business. Business develops major policies and programs and commits capital only after research points the way. As a graduate who has earned a degree in a business discipline, you will be expected to know how to conduct such research. While the emphasis of this book is on the student researcher, it is important for you to realize that research skills are vital to business success.

Technology may have changed the manner in which modern research is conducted, but the essential process remains the same today. Whether conducted by a medieval student of theology, a modern business person, or a twentieth century marketing major at an Ivy League school, the same basic steps need to be followed.

Eight Steps to Conducting Research

1. Identifying a topic or problem to be solved.
2. Formulating a thesis or purpose statement.
3. Clarifying the purpose of your paper and choosing appropriate research strategies.
4. Investigating and reading sources.
5. Collecting information relevant to your purpose.
6. Critically evaluating and analyzing data so that conclusions may be reached.
7. Organizing material, writing about it in a clear and effective style.
8. Documenting sources from which information has been taken.

Another difference between our medieval academic and today's student is that more often in the past, the subject matter of scholarly research was theology, philosophy, and science. While considerable research still goes on in liberal arts disciplines, more and more today, the business of academic research is business itself.

The reasons for this are fundamentally economic. Our service- and information-based economies require larger numbers of the population to be educated to perform specific occupations. No longer is the college or university a place to go just to acquire a general education. There is too much to learn now. Rather, higher education has become the route to occupational success. Surveys of recent incoming freshmen classes confirm these attitudes. According to the Cooperative Institutional Research Program of the American Council of Education, "business is still the most preferred career among college freshmen, (23.6%—1988) and being very well off financially is one of the top personal goals of first year students (75.6%—1987)."

1.2 WHAT IS BUSINESS RESEARCH?

Economists define *business* as the complete system of enterprises that participate in the manufacturing and marketing of goods and services to consumers. In practical terms, *business* produces, distributes, and maintains the products and services a society uses. Business operates within different economic and political systems, which often determine how transactions are carried out.

American business people operate within a mixed-capitalistic economy and a democratic political system. It follows that our conduct of business is very different from that in China, which follows a socialistic economic ideology and a totalitarian political system.

Business can be further classified into many different types. Students aspire to careers in these business categories and choose their major courses of study accordingly. Shown below are the business majors and career choices most in demand.

*BUSINESS MAJORS AND CAREER CHOICES

Accounting	Equine Business Management
Advertising and Public Relations	Fashion Merchandising
Banking and Finance	Retail Merchandise Management
Business Management and	Labor and Industrial Relations
Administration	Office Management
Computer Programming	Sales Management
Information Systems and	Real Estate and Insurance
Sciences	Culinary Arts
Systems Analysis	Food Service Management
Data Processing Technology	Recreation and Tourism
Computer Operating	Secretarial Studies
Data Systems Repair	Recreation/Leisure Management
Food Marketing	Transportation and Public
Marketing	Utilities
Entrepreneurship	Travel-Tourism
Hotel and Restaurant	
Management	

*List is not intended to be all-inclusive, but it does cover a broad range of possible choices.

Examples of possible topic choices for each of the above majors are listed in Chapter 2. For instance, an accounting major might choose to explore U.S. tax laws to see how they compare with other countries' tax systems while an advertising major may wish to research the effectiveness of subliminal advertising techniques.

Another distinguishing characteristic of business research is the practical preparation it affords students for their later careers. American corporations depend heavily on research in their decision- making process. The extent of this dependence can be seen in the approximately twenty billion dollars spent each year on research and development. Research and development can be seen as the engine which makes the American economy run. Whether it is a feasibility study that precedes construction of new facilities or a marketing survey that projects the success or failure of a new product, research-generated information is the basis for most business decisions. Knowing this, students who aspire to business success need to take advantage of the opportunity to become skilled researchers. They will most certainly be called on often to use these same skills during their careers. Those students who treat the business research paper as a dry, academic exercise miss the point completely. Business research papers are "experiential" exercises. The real value of the exercise is in the doing or "experiencing" of the exercise itself.

This close connection to the real business world sometimes pays unexpected dividends. Students who get involved in a business topic naturally develop some interest and expertise in that subject which may affect career choices or later investments. This is particularly true of students who have the entrepreneurial spirit and who know that a creative idea sufficiently nurtured may grow into a worthwhile business venture.

1.3 THE ENTREPRENEUR AS BUSINESS RESEARCHER

One of the enduring images on the American scene is that of the small child selling cold lemonade to thirsty passersby on a warm summer's day. The lemonade stand is testimony to the fact that in our capitalistic economy we admire the entrepreneurial spirit and encourage it in our young. Many of the fortunes made during the technological explosion of the second half of this century were made by individuals applying the lesson of the lemonade stand (identifying a product or service for which there is a need) to other areas of business.

This rise of the entrepreneur has received considerable public attention. Major corporations specifically encourage their employees to emulate the creative risk-taking of the entrepreneur. Some colleges and universities offer courses and/or majors in entrepreneurship. More and more students envision themselves as someday running their own business rather than choosing a corporate track. They are motivated by success stories such as that of Frederick W. Smith, founder and chief executive officer of Federal Express. Inevitably, when students read about successful entrepreneurs, they learn that the success story more often than not had its beginning in an idea that was completely and thoroughly researched before any action was taken.

The story of Fred Smith and Federal Express confirms the potential value of research. As a student at Yale, Smith first wrote about his idea for a package delivery service in a research paper for an economics class. The paper received a "C" from his professor, who clearly had little confidence in Smith's idea.

Years later, in 1973, Smith risked his own capital (eight and a half million) and raised an additional seventy million by persuading financiers that his idea would work. Today, Federal Express employs nearly eighty thousand employees and has approximately six billion dollars in annualized revenues. As a major stockholder, Fred Smith is one of the wealthiest men in the United States. Smith's comments on his success are instructive. He explains how his vision, grounded in his research at Yale, has made him a most successful corporate entrepreneur:

> ... My definition of an entrepreneur is more attuned to someone ... purpose-driven. He or she has a specific objective to accomplish. In that respect, I'm an entrepreneur, but I'm a professional business manager as

Smith's delivery empire began as a college paper, followed by careful research and planning.

well.... My belief was that the world—or at that time, the United States—needed this very different type of logistical system. I was absolutely certain about it, and I had a specific plan for how that system should be built and developed. It was that vision that was the primary driving force. ("Business Strategy" 18).

Not every success story that begins with research is a Federal Express blockbuster. Research is equally essential to small business entrepreneurs with more modest dreams. As a student at Bowling Green University, Jeff Metzger began exploring the success of upscale gourmet ice cream franchises. What Jeff learned as part of a research paper project led directly to his starting Lord's Creamery, a small retail outlet in the Cincinnati area whose first year sales exceeded a quarter of a million dollars. This early success has led to further research aimed at evaluating alternative ways to expand the business.

Not all business research is entrepreneurial. Most students graduating with business degrees will go to work for corporations. In these corporate settings, they will be asked to search out information, solve problems, and analyze situations to provide a basis for decisions.

1.4 TYPES OF BUSINESS RESEARCH PAPERS

You may have to write different types of papers. Your instructor may be very specific when assigning a research project. This will simplify matters for you. However, since you probably will write a number of research papers for different instructors and use research throughout your career, you need to be able to differentiate between research papers' two basic purposes.

The Informational Paper

The purpose of the informational paper is to explain or reveal a topic. Facts or issues are presented in a straightforward manner designed to increase the reader's understanding of the meaning or significance of your subject.

"Disease Of the Year: Illness as Glitch," an article written for the January 1989 issue of *Discover* magazine, is primarily informational. In it, Shawna Vogel, the author, takes her readers through a detailed *analysis* or *explanation* of computer viruses. She refrains from taking a position or trying to persuade. When you begin work on a research paper, you must clearly understand your primary purpose. Notice the informative tone of Shawna Vogel's article in the following excerpt.

> The sad truth is that there can be no complete protection from computer viruses. If human beings were to live as hermits, in a kind of protective quarantine, they would be a lot less prone to infection, but they would also get a lot less done. The same is true of computers. If they are to achieve their full potential as helpmates, they have to be in communication. And as long as they communicate, sharing data and programs, they will be vulnerable to viral attack. "Our ability to protect ourselves will remain limited as long as sharing continues," says Wilson. "The more you share code, the more of a threat viruses become. But that's the kind of environment people want to move into" (Vogel 66).

The Analytical/Persuasive Paper

By contrast, the purpose of the analytical/persuasive paper is not so much to explain and inform but to arrive at conclusions based on an evaluation of the facts. Analytical/persuasive papers may be argumentative in that their primary purpose is to convince an audience to accept your point of view. This type of paper is the most traditional research paper assignment, as it demands the most of the student. Not only must you identify or define the problem and thoroughly research it, you must also arrive at conclusions and justify them by logically presenting evidence. This exercise in analysis and persuasion is a sophisticated and challenging intellectual exercise.

An article published in the March 1988 issue of *Administrative Management* is a clear example of analysis and persuasion based on research. Entitled "Don't Wait Until You Get Burned," the article argues that computer fraud and theft have become such a serious threat that companies must invest in security measures for self-protection. The author, Douglas Finlay, uses evidence gathered by interviews to convincingly make his case. Note the tone of the concluding paragraphs from Finlay's article.

Applying the Proper Amount

No information security system is foolproof. There are those employees with malicious intent who will work to discover a weakness not hitherto found. But security models and products are a precious deterrent to continual breaches. They provide you with an organized and systematic front against employees and others whose devious behavior cannot be contained by moral or ethical wisdoms. Management cannot be too cautious at the same time in favor of security. With the object to enact the proper amount of deterrence, you must take care that the deterrence will pay—and not cost—in the long haul. A "gung-ho" attitude to apply security technology at every turn in the company may create only a sense of false security. Don't get "burned" by that, too (Finlay 22).

1.5 A BUSINESS RESEARCHER'S JOURNAL

There are two preliminary steps to take before beginning a research project. The first is to purchase a notebook exclusively for recording ideas, notes, and any other information related to your topic. This is your research journal. Consider it the place to keep all project-related materials. When you keep your work in one place, you reduce chances of loss. More importantly, use the journal to practice writing and to generate fresh insights about your subject. The best way to do this is to freewrite.

Writing regularly prepares you to write your best in much the same way that daily tennis workouts ready a player for an important match. Effective writing is just as important to the success of the research paper as the research itself. The journal is the place to get that needed practice. Because of the nature of freewriting, it also stimulates creative understanding.

Freewriting is unstructured writing. Your primary concern should not be spelling, mechanics, and grammar, but getting the thoughts in your head down on paper. You may wish to start with questions about your topic. Answer your own questions and follow any other directions your ideas may take you. Talk to yourself. Brainstorm possibilities, however farfetched they may seem. React to things you read or watch on television that connect to your topic.

Here are two student examples of how questions might lead to a freewriting exercise that can generate fresh insights.

Ask Yourself These Questions

1. How do products from Japan compare with American made products?
2. What is competition in the global marketplace?
3. What are the consequences for working-class America of the American economy's decline?

4. How must the U.S. economy be restructured if it is to regain its position as a world business leader?
5. What is the impact of the technological revolution on the global economy? What effect has it on the domestic market?

Freewriting: The American Economy

Is America losing its position as leader in the global marketplace? How valid is this view? Imports from the Far East have weakened the American economy. I know that many Japanese products are superior to American made products. What happened to the "buy American" campaign? Have Americans forgotten the importance of buying American made products? I find it disturbing that Japan manufactures better automobiles, televisions, and computers than Americans do. Should we simply accept that America is declining as a world power? I want to know more about the history of the American economy. At the end of World War II, American technology was ahead of other countries'. It seems that since the Vietnam War, the United States has been going downhill rapidly. At one time we were the biggest creditor nation; now we are the biggest debtor. What happened to our manufacturing capabilities? Are we focusing too much on service industries? What kind of effect has this decline on the working class? Will we ever be able to bring back the past when business was the business of the American people?

Ask Yourself These Questions

1. How does the present attitude toward senior citizens compare with the attitude in the past?
2. What is old age? Is it how you feel or how many years you have lived?
3. What effect will an older consumer population have on advertising and marketing?
4. How will factors of health, wealth, and life experience of the elderly contribute to their lifestyle?
5. What impact will the age revolution have on social change in America?

Freewriting: The Age Revolution

People in their mature years are getting more attention today than they did not too long ago, when our country was obsessed with youth. We are becoming a nation of middle-aged people. Is this the baby boom generation moving into retirement? How do we define old? I observe that many of the negative stereotypes about older people are changing. The media portray positive images of older actors and actresses. For example, the popular TV comedies show older women who are active and enjoy life. With modern medical technology, older people are enjoying improved health. I observe more seniors walking, jogging, and golfing. If the elderly are retired, healthy, and affluent, what goods and services will they be looking for? This will be a big challenge to marketers. They won't need the basics. I think leisure businesses such as travel and hospitality industries will mushroom. Is age discrimination an issue? Fast-food establishments are hiring retired workers. Recently I saw an advertisement that Holiday Inn will sponsor athletes at the National Senior Olympic games. The old-timers are going for gold.

Of course, your research journal is also the place to do preliminary outlines, plan your search strategy, collect articles from current newspapers and magazines, and keep notes from your library reading. If you use the journal for all of these purposes, it will serve you well in developing and finalizing your final paper.

1.6 THE RESEARCHER'S SCHEDULE

The second preliminary step you need to take is develop a detailed work schedule for each phase of your research paper. Research papers, theses, or dissertations are large, challenging assignments which can threaten and discourage an already overloaded student. The most effective way to accomplish these tasks is to establish a timetable of intermediate deadlines. Instead of thinking about the entire assignment, set your mind on meeting each intermediate deadline. If you are able to take this approach—one step at a time—you will finish the entire task and on time.

Before setting up your schedule consider these factors. What are your other current commitments? What hours are devoted to classes, study, or work? Whether or not you have a formal time-management plan, you will have to integrate your research schedule with your existing obligations. How many hours per day can you devote to your project? How many days per week? What are your personal work habits? Do you work better in frequent, short spurts, or are you more effective during longer, less frequent sessions? Finally, the key question: How long do you estimate the project will take? Short research papers may be completed in four to six weeks, while dissertations often take a year or longer. Once you have answered these and other questions, you can create your own research schedule.

Start your project schedule by filling in backwards all known due dates. You will have been given the final due date and, depending on the class and your instructor, you may also have received dates by which you must submit a topic, a working bibliography, notes, and a first draft. Fill in all other dates, keeping in mind these suggestions:

1. Complete your research at least three to four weeks *before* final due date.
2. Allow one to two weeks to revise your completed first draft.

3. Plan to have final keying and proofreading done during the week preceding your final due date.

A sample researcher's work schedule follows.

RESEARCHER'S WORK SCHEDULE

TASK	DATE
1. Organizing researcher's journal	_____
2. Choosing a subject/beginning preliminary reading	_____
3. Refining the topic	_____
4. Narrowing topic to working thesis/problem	_____
5. Gathering information	_____
6. Compiling a working bibliography	_____
7. Evaluating sources	_____
8. Revising the thesis/problem sentence	_____
9. Writing the outline	_____
10. Scheduling field interviews	_____
11. Conducting surveys	_____
12. Completing reading and notetaking	_____
13. Preparing charts and/or graphs	_____
14. Writing the first draft	_____
15. Editing the first draft	_____
16. Rewriting the edited draft	_____
17. Preparing the list of works cited	_____
18. Assembling the final paper	_____
19. Proofreading the final paper	_____
20. Submitting the final paper	_____

Application Activities

1. Organize your researcher's journal and make your initial written entry.
2. Complete your researcher's schedule on the back inside cover of this book.
3. Listed below are some industries dominated by entrepreneurial companies. Select one industry and find out what entrepreneurial process was involved in launching that company.
   a. Computer industry
   b. Telecommunication industry
   c. Hotel chains
   d. Motion pictures industry
   e. Fast-food restaurants
4. Compare and contrast the characteristics of an informational paper with those of an analytical/persuasive paper.

2
PREPARING TO BEGIN RESEARCH

Learning Objectives

Upon completing this chapter you should be able to:

1. Select a broad business subject for your research paper or business report.
2. Narrow the broad subject to a specific topic.
3. Clarify the primary purpose for the paper.
4. Write a preliminary thesis/purpose statement.
5. Write a preliminary outline.

2.1 BUILDING A RESEARCH PLAN

If you have been assigned a traditional research paper by your instructor, your plan will begin differently than if you are required to write a business report that needs to be researched. For the research paper, you will need to select a topic, while for business reports requiring research you must identify and analyze a problem. With this in mind, begin your planning by thinking through the entire project. One way to do that is to answer the following questions:

1. What background information (economic, social, historical, etc.) is relevant to your topic or problem?
2. Is the purpose of your assignment informational or analytical/persuasive?
3. Who is your audience? Are you writing just for your instructor, or is there a larger audience assumed?

4. What kinds of information will you need to accomplish your purpose?
5. What are likely to be the best sources for this information?
6. What research methods will be needed to obtain this information?
7. How will you evaluate or analyze the information obtained?
8. What will be your point of view towards your topic, or what kind of conclusions are you likely to draw?

Your answers to these questions are important because they provide a general overview of the project. Now you can begin more specific preparatory steps.

2.2 SELECTING A TOPIC/IDENTIFYING A PROBLEM

You will benefit the most from doing research about a topic in which you have personal interest. This personal interest generates enthusiasm which, in turn, motivates you to learn all there is to know about a topic. This enthusiasm or desire may result from a number of reasons. Here are three:

1. Your topic relates to your major course of study in which you have a strong interest.
2. You have been thinking about eventual career choices and believe your topic may help you make a better decision.
3. You have an entrepreneurial interest in your topic. You see yourself as someday beginning a business or making an investment in this area.

Since enthusiasm, desire, and interest are all vital to the success of a business research paper, you should begin your thinking by considering a topic that falls into one of these three scenarios.

Before you proceed in the selection process, ask yourself the following questions to avoid common student pitfalls:

1. Will the topic you are considering meet with your instructor's approval? If in doubt, check.
2. Is your topic timely, or has it been worked over too many times?
3. Are you capable of handling the topic, or is it of a technical nature that is beyond your available time or expertise?
4. Will you be able to obtain sufficient quality information in order to fulfill your purpose? If you are uncertain, a research librarian should be able to answer your questions.
5. Does your assignment ask you to write a business report that requires research? If so, be certain your topic allows you to identify a problem or need.

To help facilitate the selection process, consult the appropriate lists below, each of which contains broad subject areas which need to be narrowed to more specific topics.

ACCOUNTING

Accounting Management
Accounts Receivable
American Credit
Amortization
Automation Auditing
Certified Public Accountants
Computerized Payroll System
Depreciation
Evolution of Accounting
Federal Reserve System

Foreign Exchange Accounting
Hospitality Accounting
Income Accounting
Inventory Loans
Liquidation
Non-Profit Organizations
Public Accounting Profession
Sales Accounting
Tax Consultants
Taxation in the USA

ADMINISTRATIVE AND OFFICE SYSTEMS

Bilingual Secretary
Business Data Communications
Changing Office Workplace
Clerical Employment
Electronic Mail
Ergonomics
Executive Assistant
Intercultural Communications
Office Administrator
Office Etiquette
Office Politics

Professional Development
Professional Secretaries International
Quality of Worklife
Secretarial & Business Service
Secretarial Profession in the
    21st Century
Secretary as Manager
The Secretary/Boss Team
Supervising Personnel
Telephone Technology
Word Processing Software

ADVERTISING

Advertising Agencies
Art Directors
Brand Names
Brand Rivalry
Broadcast Advertising
Buyer Behavior
Celebrity Testimonials
Consumer Research
Cooperative Advertising
Copy Writers

Direct Mail Advertising
Effie Awards
Ethnic Stereotypes
Evolution of Advertising
How Women are Depicted in
    Television Advertising
Print Advertising
Product Positioning
Subliminal Advertising
Truth in Advertising

BUSINESS EDUCATION

Back to Basics Movement
Career Education
Classroom Management
Competency Test for Teachers
Cost of Higher Education
Cultural Literacy
Education for Managers
Employability Skills
Entrepreneurial Education
Future of Business Education

Illiteracy
Information Era
International Issues
Interviewing Skills
Japan's School System
Listening Skills for Business
Methodologies for the 1990s
Nonverbal Communication
Preparing Business Teachers
Professional Organizations

Guidance

Teaching Standards for the 21st
 Century
Team Teaching

COMPUTER INFORMATION SERVICES

Artificial Intelligence
Automation
Computer Equipment
Computer Fraud
Computer Languages
Computer Software
Computerized Factories
Desktop Publishing
Evolution of Computers
Hardware

Microchips Industry
Microcomputer Graphics
Newest Computer Generation
Online Databases
Optical Discs
Pioneers of Computer Industry
Portable Computers
Satellite Videoconferencing
Telecommuting and the Future
Voice Input

CULINARY ARTS

American Regional Cooking
Appetizers
Asian Cooking
Baked Goods
Buffets
Cake Decorating
Canning
Confectionery
Dairy Products
Entertaining
Entrees

European Cookery
Gourmet Cookery
Herbs
International Cookery
Italian Cookery
Jewish Cookery
Outdoor Cookery
Seafood
Spanish Cookery
Vegetable Cookery
Wines

ECONOMICS

American Capitalism
Bushonomics
Discretionary Spending of the Elderly
Economic Change in the Soviet Union
Foreign Aid
Inflation in the United States
International Economics
Japanese Economic System
Keynesian Theories of Employment
Migrant Workers

Minimum Wage Laws
National Debt
Perestroika in the Soviet Union
Poverty in the United States
Rural Economics: The Farm Problem
Social Security Benefits and
 the Future
The Great Depression
United States and Soviet Relations
Urban Economics: The Problem of
 the Cities
Welfare

FINANCE/REAL ESTATE

Banks
Brokers
Capital Market
Condominiums
Corporation Reports

Inflation
Insurance Companies
International Finance
Investments
Loans

Credit
Estate Planning
Finance Companies
Financial Disclosure
Financial Executives
Financial Planning
Foreign Ownership
Housing Developers

Money Market
Mortgages
Multiple Listing
Property Management
Real Estate Agents
Real Estate Law
Real Estate Loans
Rental Property

FOOD SERVICE

Beverage Management
California's Champagne Industry
Careers in Food Service
Computers in the Food
  Service Industry
Concession Management
Equipment for Food

Ethnic Foods in America
Ethnic Restaurants
Fast-Food Chains
Future of Food Service Industry
Health Foods

History of Coffee Trends
Home Delivery of Foods
Imported Wine Coolers
Menu Designing and Marketing
Merchandising
Natural Foods and Herbs
Nutrition
Premium Beers
Sanitation Procedures in
  Food Preparation

Sugar Susbstitutes
U.S. Wines

HEALTH AND HUMAN SERVICES

AIDS Research
Careers in Social Work
Exercise Personnel
Food Labels
Health Care Administration
Health Products
Health Resorts
Industrial Hygienist
Industrial Nursing
Mental Health

Medical Personnel
Nursing Administration
Occupational Therapist
Paraprofessionals in Social Work
Physical Fitness Centers
Public Health
Public Health Nursing
Social Work in Industry
Social Work with Minorities
Welfare Work in Industry

HOSPITALITY

Automated Beverage Service
Bed and Breakfast Management
Catering Industry
Chain Operations
Conventions and Tradeshows
Employee Benefit Programs
Employee Turnover
Fast-Food Industry
Food and Beverage Management
Health Facilities

Hotels in the Soviet Union
Hotel Mergers
Leaders of the Hospitality Industry
McDonalds Corporation
Menu Planning
Older Workers
Theft
Vending Machines
Video Checkout Systems
Women in Hospitality Management

MANAGEMENT

Employee Absenteeism
Evolution of Benefits
Feminine Management Style
Flex-Time Workweek
High Tech Businesses
International Business
Inventory Control
Japanese Management Style
Labor Policies
Lie Detectors

Middle Management Positions
Motivating Employees
On-Site Child Care Facilities
Selective Hiring
Silicon Valley
Small Business Management
Steel Collar Workers: Robotics
Women Entrepreneurs
Work-Related Stress
Working Mothers

MARKETING

Corporate Values
Ethics & Social Responsibility
Franchising
Global Markets
Graying of America
Hispanic Market
Home Video Market
Japanese Corporations
Mail Order Selling
Market Research

Marketing to Career Women
Marketing to Children
Marketing Strategies
Marketing to the Baby Boomers
Niche Marketing
Selling of Lifestyles
Telecommunications
Target Marketing
Taste Testing
Transcultural Marketing

RETAILING

Advertising
Catalog Shopping
Changing Styles in Fashion
Competition
Credit Cards
Customer Service
Department Stores
Designer Labels
Discount Stores
Fashion Trends in the
    Twenties

Fraud and the Mail Order Business
Jeans Industry
Leading American Designers
Leading European Designers
(800) Number and Selling
Retail Theft
Self-Service and the Consumer
Shopping Malls
Sportswear Industry
Window Displays

TRAVEL/TOURISM

Airports
Carnival Cruise Lines
Charter Flights
Club Mediterranean
Corporate Travel Management
Deregulation of Airlines
Domestic Travel
Foreign Travel
Frequent-Flier Programs

Origins of the Cruise Industry
People Express Airlines
The Car Rental Industry
The Railroad Industry
The Role of the Meeting Planners
Thomas Cook
Trade Shows and Exhibitions
Travel Management Services
Travelers' Checks

Identifying a Problem

Approach topic selection for the business report that requires research differently. While your general topic may come from the preceding lists, you must identify a problem in your topic area that needs solving. Next, you must systematically investigate the situation, using the most appropriate research methods. Collect and organize the information so that it may be evaluated. Evaluate the evidence you have gathered and draw logical conclusions. Depending on the nature of the business situation, you might then have to make recommendations, which you would include in a written business report.

The example cited in Chapter 1 (1.3) is a clear example of a business report that requires research. Jeff Metzger studied the upscale gourmet ice cream market, using both secondary and primary research techniques. He read the literature available from companies and interviewed owners of franchises in the Cincinnati area. After graduating with an MBA from Bowling Green, Jeff used the academic research he had done to solve the "problem" of starting his own business. The report he had written as a graduate student became a successful reality.

2.3 NARROWING YOUR SCOPE

Once you have selected a broad subject for your inquiry, you need to move to a more specific issue that will be your topic. If your field of interest is food service, you may wish to research "Fast-Food Chains" or, you may further narrow your topic by selecting "Opportunities in Pizza Franchising." How much you narrow your general subject will depend on the requirements of your assignment. An eight- to ten-page research paper for a first-year composition class will call for a topic that is considerably more narrowed than a topic for a thirty-page graduate assignment.

The place to begin narrowing your topic is the library. If your broad subject of interest is "Advertising," look that subject up in several different encyclopedias. Though encyclopedias are rarely used as major sources of information in college research, they are useful starting points. This preliminary reading gives you a general overview of the topic and at the same time breaks down advertising into a number of subheadings.

Another effective narrowing technique is to continue your library exploration by checking the online subject or author search for a book that treats your subject generally. *Ogilvy on Advertising* is such a book. If you scan the table of contents and the index of this type of book you can choose from a large number of specific topics that fall under the subject of advertising.

Another useful approach to narrowing your topic is to first link your general subject with a related subject to create new possibilities:

- advertising for children
- color in magazine advertising
- advertising and celebrity testimonials
- cost of different types of advertising
- market research and advertising

Having created some new concepts through this linking technique, select one that interests you most and begin brainstorming by posing a series of questions. For example, linking color and magazine advertising might raise these points:

- Does color add appeal to the magazine advertisement?
- How does the cost of color compare to the cost of black and white?
- Does color influence the emotional reaction of consumers?
- What products are best suited to color ads?

Use your research journal to record your narrowing exercises. This process will bring you closer to understanding what the purpose of your paper is and will help you formulate a preliminary thesis/purpose statement.

2.4 CLARIFYING YOUR PURPOSE

Once you have narrowed your topic to fit the scope of the assignment, check again to see if you are absolutely clear about the primary purpose of your paper. Is it informational or analytical/persuasive?

It may be that your instructor will resolve this question for you by requiring a basic informational paper. Or, you may be asked to write the more traditional undergraduate research paper in which you need to support a thesis with evidence from research. Such an analytical/persuasive paper will require you to use specific techniques to convince your audience to accept your thesis.

However, business topics often lend themselves to pure analysis and have become much more common in today's business curricula. In such cases, you will be writing an analytical business report in which you research and identify a problem to offer solutions and recommendations.

You must be absolutely clear about your purpose, because:

1. When you are unclear about your purpose for writing the paper, your audience is likely to come away with a similarly vague, uncertain reaction.

2. Analytical/persuasive papers require different developmental writing techniques than informational papers. Being certain of your purpose allows you to consciously choose the most appropriate techniques.

3. Clarity of purpose will also lead logically to an effective thesis/purpose statement.

2.5 WRITING A PRELIMINARY THESIS/PURPOSE STATEMENT

You may recall from earlier writing courses that a thesis states the controlling or central point of your paper. It is likely you were first taught this concept before writing a short composition, such as a five-paragraph essay. Writing a thesis in such a context was relatively simple. If, for example, you believed that the death penalty should be abolished, you said so directly in the first paragraph, offered your evidence in the next three paragraphs, and concluded by repeating your thesis in the fifth paragraph.

Writing a thesis/purpose statement for a business research paper is not so simple. Research is a dynamic process of discovery during which the way you think or feel about your topic may change. That is why you need to write a *preliminary* thesis/purpose statement, which may be altered by the research process itself. The preliminary thesis/purpose statement then, is a starting point which represents your thinking at the beginning of the project. In this sense, it is similar to a hypothesis in the scientific method. You still need to have your thesis confirmed by the evidence. If your research takes you in a different direction, you may need to refine your final thesis or change it altogether. For example, if you began with the hypothesis that a quick way to become wealthy is to invest in commodities, you might write this preliminary thesis/purpose statement:

Every investor should include commodities in a well-rounded investment portfolio.

Once you researched your topic thoroughly, you might uncover information that would lead to a different conclusion:

Commodities are a high risk investment and should be avoided by the average investor.

Then again, it is entirely possible that your research will confirm your preliminary thesis, and it will remain intact as your final thesis.

Try to keep your statement simple and clear. Do this by writing your thesis in one sentence whenever possible and by using specific language that avoids vague generalities.

INFORMATIONAL PRELIMINARY THESIS

Specific: The use of color in print advertising has proven more effective than black and white ads.

Vague: Some advertising techniques can be very successful.

Specific: Bo Jackson and Michael Jordan are examples of celebrity athletes who have made most effective television ads.

Vague: Celebrities are often effective in certain types of advertising.

Of course, the way you word your thesis statement will depend directly on your purpose. For an analytical/persuasive paper, you make an assertion about your topic and defend it by argumentation.

ANALYTICAL/PERSUASIVE PRELIMINARY THESIS

Analytical/Persuasive: Corporations need to install comprehensive security systems to protect against computer fraud and theft.

A purely analytical purpose requires that you state the central idea as a solution to a problem or recommendation.

Analytical: To protect against computer fraud and theft, XYZ Company should install comprehensive security systems.

Remember that your preliminary thesis is a concise statement of what you set out to prove or analyze. Such statements provide a focus which keeps you from straying from your topic. Avoid writing repetitious statements such as "This paper will explore...," or "The purpose of this paper is to..." Just get straight to the point as shown in the above examples.

2.6 WRITING A PRELIMINARY OUTLINE

If the preliminary thesis/purpose statement is the point of departure for your research journey, the preliminary outline can be thought of as a rough map, a way to see the likely direction your paper will take. It is too early for the map to be very detailed, since you have not yet begun your research. That will come later when you complete a final outline in the prewriting stage (see Chapter 8).

The best way to construct a preliminary outline is to create a three-part structure based on the ancient Aristotelian rule: "All good writing contains a beginning, a middle, and an end." Set up this traditional outline and then fill in your ideas as they exist now in the order that seems most logical. Arrange your items so that minor ideas precede major ones. Keep in mind that this preliminary outline will be filled in with considerably more detail after you have researched your topic.

One hotel food and beverage management major at a northeastern university conceived the idea of writing a short analytical/persuasive paper about how to start a food catering business. Using the Aristotelian three-part structure, the student composed the following preliminary outline.

Starting A Food Catering Business

INTRODUCTION

Vision of Successful Catering Business
Thesis Statement

MIDDLE

Characteristics of a Caterer
Market Research
Deciding What Services to Offer
Marketing Your Business
Setting Prices
Financial and Legal Considerations
Package Plans
Budgeting and Shakedown Period

CONCLUSION

Summary
Motivational Statement

Notice how the preliminary outline lacks specific detail. This is as it should be. For a look at how this same outline appears in final form, look ahead to Chapter 7.

Application Activities

1. Explain two different ways to begin narrowing a broad, comprehensive subject to a more specific topic.
2. Describe two possible scenarios in your future business career in which you would have to do the following:
   a. Research and write an informational report.
   b. Research and write an analytical report.
3. Choose five general topics from section 2.2; narrow each one and write a thesis/purpose sentence suitable for an 8–10 page analytical/persuasive paper.

A. GENERAL TOPIC:

   NARROWED TOPIC:

   THESIS/PURPOSE STATEMENT:

B. GENERAL TOPIC:

   NARROWED TOPIC:

   THESIS/PURPOSE STATEMENT:

C. GENERAL TOPIC:

   NARROWED TOPIC:

   THESIS/PURPOSE STATEMENT:

D. GENERAL TOPIC:

NARROWED TOPIC:

THESIS/PURPOSE STATEMENT:

E. GENERAL TOPIC:

NARROWED TOPIC:

THESIS/PURPOSE STATEMENT:

4. Explain the difference between a preliminary outline and a final outline.

3

COLLECTING INFORMATION FOR THE RESEARCH PAPER

Learning Objectives

Upon completing this chapter you should be able to:

1. Explain how a library is organized.
2. Locate books using the Dewey Decimal system and the Library of Congress system.
3. Use either the traditional card catalog or a computerized catalog in the research process.
4. Locate information in both general and specialized business references.
5. Use the computerized system Infotrac to retrieve bibliographic references.

3.1 USING THE LIBRARY AS A RESOURCE

A bargain is defined as something of value you are able to acquire at an advantageous price. As a student interested in a business career, you should realize that libraries may be the most underrated bargain of our times. They certainly fit the definition well enough. They are generally available to you at little or no cost, and the potential value libraries hold for you may be beyond calculation. The comments of two respected thinkers support this idea:

Next to acquiring good friends the best acquisition is that of good books.
Charles Caleb Colton

A great library contains the diary of the human race. The great consulting room of a wise man is a library.

George Dawson

Surprisingly, libraries can be threatening, unfamiliar territory for the uninitiated. This unfamiliarity results both in wasted time and effort as well as unsuccessful information searches.

The purpose of this chapter is to totally familiarize you with a library's workings so you can gather information, save time, and earn good grades. Once this happens, the library will be a comfortable place you can visit over and over again.

You may do so for pure enjoyment, or to obtain information for a crucial business decision. At present you need to understand how to use the library because it is the logical starting point for virtually all research projects.

3.2 UNDERSTANDING LIBRARY ORGANIZATION

A library is a collection of books, periodicals, newspapers, and other informative materials which are systematically organized for ease of reference. The sooner you learn the organizational scheme of the library, the sooner you will be able to tap all that the library has to offer. It is the organizational scheme which can make your research easier. Here is a typical station-by-station library arrangement that you are likely to encounter.

Library Stations

Main Circulation Desk: The main desk is where you charge out or return books or other materials. General information about library services is available here. This station usually is near the major entrance.

Card Catalog: All books and other materials in the library are listed alphabetically, usually on index cards. Many libraries have computerized card catalogs to increase ease of access, or are in the process of doing so.

Stacks: The open stacks are the shelves where books are arranged according to call numbers. You may look for a specific book that you found listed in the card catalog or just browse through an entire section of related titles.

Reserved Reading: Professors often set aside works to be read in their classes. These books may be held at a reserve desk or in a reserve reading room. Some libraries allow overnight borrowing of reserve books, while others restrict use to the library.

Reference Room: This station houses major research references such as encyclopedias, bibliographic dictionaries, and atlases. Here is where you can search general and specialized business indexes. Many libraries may have reference librarians who offer personal assistance.

Periodicals Section: Current periodicals are shelved here. Back volumes may also be bound and stored chronologically in the periodicals room or kept on microforms. The most common microforms are microfiche and microfilm, which store miniaturized reproductions of printed material—books, newspapers, and periodicals. To use microforms, you must have a reader, a machine that enlarges print.

Audiovisual Station: Many libraries contain media sections which have films, videotapes, and microfilms. These nonprint materials may be listed separately in an audiovisual catalog.

Electronic and Computer Research Station: At some libraries the future has arrived in the form of modern research methods that can simplify and shorten your search (See Chapter 4 on Dialog).

3.3 UNDERSTANDING TWO BOOK CLASSIFICATION SYSTEMS

Since your first research efforts will begin in the card catalog, you must learn the two keys that open the doors to the rest of the library. Those two keys are the Dewey Decimal system of book classification and the Library of Congress system. Both attempt to order and organize all recorded knowledge. Some libraries may use only one system, but it is likely that you will encounter both methods. Learning the characteristics of each will prepare you for any eventuality.

3.3.1 The Dewey Decimal System

The most widely used system was introduced in 1873 by an Amherst College student, Melvil Dewey, who wished to simplify the task of finding a book in the library stacks. The brilliance of Dewey's idea is its all-encompassing simplicity. The Dewey Decimal system divides all categories of knowledge into ten major categories, each of which is given a span of 100 numbers as follows:

Dewey Decimal Classification

000–099 General Works	500–599 Pure Science
100–199 Philosophy	600–699 Applied Science
200–299 Religion	700–799 The Arts
300–399 Social Sciences	800–899 Literature
400–499 Language	900–999 History, Travel

Each of these ten classes is further divided into ten subcategories. The most important general classes for the economics and business student researcher are the 300 and 600 groups.

The 600 group is divided as follows:

600–609 Applied Sciences	650–659 Managerial Services

610–619 Medicine
620–629 Engineering
630–639 Agriculture

640–649 Domestic Arts

660–669 Chemical Technology
670–679 Manufactures
680–689 Miscellaneous
  Manufactures
690–699 Building

The 650 group is subdivided and narrows business subjects even further.

650 Communications, Business
651 Office Economy
652 Writing, Typewriters
653 Abbreviations, Shorthand
654 Telegraph, Cables

655 Printing, Publishing
656 Transportation, Railroading
657 Bookkeeping, Accounts
658 General Business
659 Other Topics

The decimal point adds further subdivisions. For example, the 658 group is subdivided as follows:

658.1 Organization and Finance
658.2 Management of Plants
658.3 Personnel Management
658.4 Principles of Management

658.5 Management of Production
658.7 Management of Materials
658.8 Management of Distribution
658.9 Management of Specific
  Kinds of Enterprises

Some books on economics will also be found in the 300 group. For example:

332.1 Banks and Banking
332.2 Specialized Banking
  Institutions
332.3 Credit and Loan Institutions
332.4 Money
332.5 Other Mediums of Exchange

332.6 Investments
332.7 Credit
332.8 Interest and discount
332.9 Counterfeiting, Forgery

Remember that the original appeal of the Dewey Decimal system was its simplicity. This has not changed. Acquaint yourself with the ten major categories and the 100 numbers used for each. Finally, remember that the 300 and 600 groups are the general categories for most business sources.

3.3.2 The Library of Congress System

Many larger libraries now use the Library of Congress classification system. The basic advantage of this system is that by combining both letters and numbers it is able to expand infinitely the categories covered in the Dewey Decimal system. As our knowledge continues to increase at a rapid rate, this system is able to accommodate such growth.

Library of Congress Classification

The Library of Congress system divides all categories of knowledge into twenty-one major categories, each indicated by a letter of the alphabet as follows:

A. General Works
B. Philosophy, Religion, Psychology
C. History and Auxiliary Sciences
D. History: General and Old World
E-F. History: North and South America
G. Geography
H. Social Sciences, Statistics, Economics
J. Political Science
K. Law
L. Education
M. Music
N. Fine Arts
P. Language and Literature
Q. Science
R. Medicine
S. Agriculture
T. Technology
U. Military Science
V. Naval Science
Z. Bibliography and Library Science

Each category of knowledge is subdivided further by adding second letters. For example in section H, Social Sciences and Economics, the main subdivisions follow:

HB Economics
HC Economics, Economic history
HD Economics, Management
HE Transportation, Communication
HF Accounting, Advertising, Marketing
HG Finance

Each category is subdivided further by adding numbers 1–99999. For example, in the category HF—Advertising, the following subdivisions are listed:

HF—Advertising

5801	Periodicals. Societies. Serials
5802	Yearbooks
.5	Congresses
5803	Dictionaries. Encyclopedias
	Directories of advertisers and advertising agents
5084	General
	United States
5805	General
5806	By state, A–W
5807	Local, A–Z
.5	By business, A–Z 1/
5808	Other regions or countries, A–Z
	Under each country:
	.x General
	.x2 By place, A–Z
	.x3 By business, A–Z
	Biography
5810.A2A–Z	Collective
.A3–Z	Individual, A–Z
	History
5811	General works

5813	By region or country, A–Z
	Study and teaching. Research
5814	General works
5815	By region or country, A–Z
5816	Competitions. Prizes. Awards
	General works, treatises, and textbooks
	Theoretical
5821	General works
5822	Psychology of advertising
	Practical
5823	General works
5824	Office organization, accounting, etc.
5825	Advertising writing, including lay-out and typography
5826	Forms, etc.
.5	Media planning
5827	General special
.2	Comparison advertising. Positioning
.4	Cooperative advertising
.6	Corrective advertising
.8	Fraudulent advertising
5828	Point of sale advertising
.2	Data processing
.4	Advertising as a profession. Vocational guidance
5829	Juvenile works
5831	Ethics and aesthetics

Once again, the business student researcher's work may be made easier by the knowledge that the "H" category in the Library of Congress classification system will lead to the most relevant sources.

3.4 SEARCHING THE LIBRARY FOR BOOKS

3.4.1 Traditional Card Catalog

The card catalog is an alphabetical index of 3 by 5 file cards which describe all books and other materials in the library. Depending on the size of the library, you may find author, title, and subject cards alphabetically interfiled (small libraries) or filed separately according to author, title, and subject (larger libraries).

The system of alphabetizing may vary from library to library. Remember that a card catalog holds a large collection of information which requires a complex system of organization. If you have difficulty finding an entry, be sure to consult your librarian for help.

Listed here are a few examples of how entries may be alphabetized in a cataloging system:

1. WORD-BY-WORD OR LETTER-BY-LETTER.   The two systems of alphabetizing are by word or by letter. Most libraries alphabetize word by word. For example, Gross National Product will be filed before Grossinger and East India will be filed before Eastern Air Lines.

WORD-BY-WORD	LETTER-BY-LETTER
South Asia	South Asia
South Sea	Southern Pacific
Southern Pacific	South Sea
Southwest	Southwest

2. ABBREVIATIONS.   Abbreviations are usually alphabetized as if they were spelled out in full. For example, St. Lawrence (Saint Lawrence) is filed after sailing and before salaries.

3. ARTICLES. Disregard the articles *a, an,* and *the* that begin a book title. The book will be cataloged by the second word of the title. For example, *The Adaptive Corporation* would be filed under "Adaptive Corporation," and *An Inquiry into the Human Prospect* would be filed under "Inquiry into the Human Prospect."

4. TITLE PREFIXES.   Names that begin with da, du, La, van are often alphabetized as if the prefix is part of the main name. For example, DaCosta, DuBrul, LaLonde, VanFleet. Mac and Mc are often alphabetized as if both were spelled Mac. For example, McCann, McGraw, MacLeish, McMahan.

3.4.2 Card Components

There are usually at least three cards listed for each book available in the library:

1. THE AUTHOR CARD
2. THE TITLE CARD
3. THE SUBJECT CARD

Each card contains the following information:

1. CALL NUMBER: Each book has its own classification number— either Dewey Decimal or Library of Congress—book number, and author number, which tell you where the book is shelved in the library. It is important that you copy this number accurately and completely.

2. AUTHOR'S NAME: The last name of the author is entered first.

3. BOOK TITLE: The title is not underlined on a catalog card and capitalization is minimal.

4. PLACE OF PUBLICATION: The city where the book was published.

5. PUBLISHER: The publisher's name is indicated.

6. DATE OF PUBLICATION: The date may be important to you if your research requires recent sources.

7. NUMBER OF PAGES: The lower case roman numerals indicate the number of pages in the preface, followed by the number of pages in the book.

8. HEIGHT: The height of the book is expressed in centimeters.

9. SUBJECT HEADINGS: You would find this book and other books on this topic under these subject headings or "tracings."

10. LIBRARY OF CONGRESS NUMBER (LOC)
11. DEWEY DECIMAL NUMBER
12. ORDER NUMBER FOR CARDS
13. INTERNATIONAL STANDARD BOOK NUMBER

Suppose, for example, you needed to compile information on investment strategies. As a viewer of "Wall Street Week," you knew that Louis Rukeyser, the host of that weekly television show, had authored several books on the topic. If you look in the card catalog under "Rukeyser," you will find an AUTHOR CARD for each of his books held by the library. However, if you knew only the title of a book and not the author, the process is different. *How to Make Money in Wall Street* will be listed on a TITLE CARD in the card catalog. Finally, should you recall neither author nor title of book, you will find SUBJECT CARDS listed under "investments" which will direct you to *How to Make Money in Wall Street* by Louis Rukeyser as well as other material on this topic. This book will be found under the subjects "investments," "stocks," and "speculation."

3.4.3 The Call Number

The all-important link between the card catalog and the shelf location is the CALL NUMBER. The call number, which is a unique combination of the classification number, book number, and author number, directs you to the specific shelf in the stacks where your book can be found.

For example, assume you had located the card for *The Economic Institution of Capitalism* by Oliver E. Williamson. The Library of Congress call number, (located in the upper left-hand corner of the card) might be HB 99.5 .W55. Find the stacks marked HB Economics, and then locate the volume marked HB 99.5.W55. Notice that the author number (.W55) begins with the first letter of the author's last name.

3.4.4 Computerized Catalog

Many libraries have stopped cataloging books on cards and have transferred the information to a database which is a collection of printed materials that has been fed into the memory of a central computer. Although the card catalog and the computerized catalog are alike in content, the method of use has changed. The researcher requests information by keying words (i.e., author, title, subject) into a terminal and reads the informtion directly from the screen. The researcher no

Author card

Author's name ——————

```
HF          Magaziner, Ira C.
1414                The silent war / by Ira Magaziner
and
.M34        Mark Patinkin. -- New York : Random
            House, 1989
                        xii, 415 p. 25 cm
                        ISBN 0-394-56979-2

            1. Competition, International -- Case
            Studies. 2. Corporations -- United
            States -- Case Studies . I. Patikin,\
            Mark. II Title.

    HF1414.M34      338.88              88-42822
```

Title Card

Book title ——————

```
            The silent war
HF          Magaziner, Ira C.
1414                The silent war / by Ira Magaziner and
.M34        Mark Patikin. -- New York : Random
            House, 1989.
                        xii, 415 p. 25 cm.
                        ISBN 0-394-56979-2

            1. Competition, International -- Case
            Studies. 2. Corporations -- United
            States -- Case Studies . I. Patikin,\
            Mark. II Title.

    HF1414.M34      338.88              88-42822
```

Subject card

Subject headings ——————

```
            Corporations--United States--Case Studies
            The silent war
HF          Magaziner, Ira C.
1414                The silent war / by Ira Magaziner and
.M34        Mark Patikin. -- New York : Random
            House, 1989.
                        xii, 415 p. 25 cm
                        ISBN 0-394-56979-2

            1. Competition, International -- Case
            Studies. 2. Corporations -- United
            States -- Case Studies . I. Patikin,\
            Mark. II Title.

    HF1414.M34      338.88              88-42822
```

Figure 1:   Sample Author, Title and Subject cards.

36

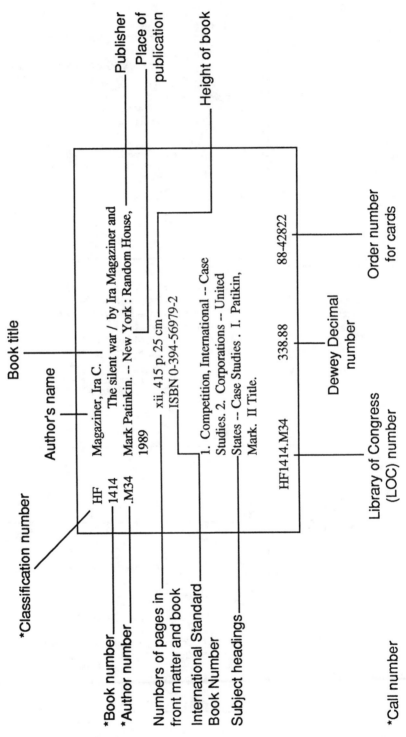

Figure 1: *continued.*

The figure shows a catalog card with the following labels and content:

- *Classification number
  - *Book number — HF
  - *Author number — 1414 / .M34
- Book title
- Author's name

Card content:
- HF
- 1414
- .M34

Magaziner, Ira C.
   The silent war / by Ira Magaziner and
Mark Patinkin. -- New York : Random House,
1989
        xii, 415 p. 25 cm
        ISBN 0-394-56979-2

        1. Competition, International -- Case
   Studies. 2. Corporations -- United
   States -- Case Studies . I. Patikin,
   Mark. II Title.

HF1414.M34   338.88   88-42822

- Publisher
- Place of publication
- Height of book
- Numbers of pages in front matter and book
- International Standard Book Number
- Subject headings
- Library of Congress (LOC) number
- Dewey Decimal number
- Order number for cards
- *Call number

longer has to look through alphabetized cards. The computer will recall printed material electronically. The first time user should ask the librarian for help or follow the instructions posted beside the terminal.

One major advantage of the computerized catalog is time saved. The computer searches through the data more quickly than you can manually search through a card catalog.

Another type of computer catalog has no keyboard terminal. Instead of typing your request on a keyboard, you touch the suitable option that is displayed on the screen. When you have found and touched your choice of author, title, or subject, the screen will show the number of records or items corresponding to your request.

This direct touch system allows you to browse, scan, scroll up, back up, and return by touching different sections of the screen.

3.5 SEARCHING THE LIBRARY FOR OTHER SOURCES

3.5.1 General Reference Works

General reference sources are often the best place to start, as they provide broad overviews of your topic. Once you discover what information is available on your subject, you can then make better choices of specialized books and periodicals.

ATLASES AND GAZETTEERS

Consult an atlas or gazetteer to find the location or boundary of a city or country.

Hammond World Atlas. Maplewood, NJ: Hammond, 1984.

New International Atlas. Rev. ed. Chicago: Rand, 1986.

Rand McNally Commercial Atlas and Marketing Guide, Chicago: Rand, 1987.

The Times Atlas of the World. 7th ed. New York: Times Books, 1985.

Webster's New Geographical Dictionary. Rev. ed Springfield: Merriam, 1984.

BIOGRAPHY

For general biographical data, consult the following works:

American Men and Women of Science. 16th ed. 8 vols. New York: Bowker, 1986.

Biographical Dictionaries: Master Index. 3 vols. Detroit: Gale, 1975.

Biography Index. New York: Wilson, 1947–.

Chambers Biographical Dictionary. Ed. J.O. Thorne and T.C. Collocott. Rev. ed. Cambridge: Cambridge UP, 1986.

Dictionary of Scientific Biography. 16 vols. New York: McGraw, 1973.

DICTIONARIES

A desk dictionary is essential to check spelling and word meanings. Use a thesaurus to choose words with closely related meanings.

McGraw-Hill Dictionary of Scientific and Technical Terms. Ed. Sybil P. Parker. 3rd. ed. New York: McGraw, 1984.

Random House Dictionary of the English Language. New York: Random, 1966.

Roget's International Thesaurus. Rev. Robert L. Canfield. 4th ed. New York: Harper, 1977.

DICTIONARIES OF QUOTATIONS

From the works listed below an appropriate quotation can be selected to introduce your paper or to dramatize a particular point.

Bartlett's Familiar Quotations. Ed. Emily Morison Beck. 15th ed. Boston: Little, 1980.

The Home Book of Quotations Classical and Modern. Ed. Burton E. Stevenson. 10th ed. New York: Dodd, 1984.

The International Thesaurus of Quotations. Ed. Rhoda T. Tripp New York: Crowell, 1970.

Quotations in Black. Ed. Anita King. Westport: Greenwood, 1981.

ENCYCLOPEDIAS

Encyclopedias, useful during the preliminary reading stage of research, give an overview of many subjects and can help you narrow your topic.

Academic American Encyclopedia. 21 vols. Danbury: Grolier, 1982.

Encyclopedia Britannica. 30 vols. 15th ed. Chicago: Encyclopedia Britain, 1984.

Encyclopedia Americana. 30 vols. New York: Americana, 1984.

International Encyclopedia of the Social Sciences. Ed. David L. Sills. 18 vols. New York: Macmillan, 1968–80.

McGraw-Hill Encyclopedia of Science and Technology. 5th ed. 15 vols. New York: McGraw, 1982.

Van Nostrand's Scientific Encyclopedia. Ed. Douglas M. Considine. 6th ed. 2 vols. New York: Van Nostrand, 1982.

GOVERNMENT PUBLICATIONS

If necessary ask the reference librarian to assist you in finding the variety of materials published by national, state, and local governments.

Guide to U.S. Government Publications. McLean, VA: Documents Index, 1973.

Statistical Reference Index. Washington: CIS, 1980.

U.S. Congress. *HR. How Our Laws Are Made.* Washington: GPO, 1981.

U.S. Department of Labor. *A Working Woman's Guide to the Job Rights.* Washington: GPO, 1988.

U.S. General Services Administration. *Doing Business With The Federal Government.* Washington: GPO, 1988.

Vertical File Index. New York: Wilson, 1935–.

READERS' GUIDE TO PERIODICAL LITERATURE

The Readers' Guide To Periodical Literature indexes 150 popular magazines. You must learn how to use the Readers' Guide because articles on business topics appear frequently in a variety of magazines. Once you have learned how articles are entered in the Readers' Guide (see Figure 2), you will be able to better utilize the specialized business indexes that are mentioned in this book.

INDEXES

The indexes to periodicals are reference works that will direct you to the most recent sources needed for your research work. Very often, periodicals provide the latest data not available in books (see Figure 3).

Applied Science and Technology Index. New York: Wilson, 1985.

Index to Periodical Articles By and About Blacks. Boston: G. K. Hall, 1973.

Magazine Index. Menlo Park, CA: Information Assess, 1976–.

National Newspaper Index. Menlo Park, CA: Information Access, 1976–.

New York Times Index. New York: New York Times, 1913–.

Newspaper Index. Wooster, OH: Bell, 1972–.

Readers' Guide to Periodical Literature. New York: Wilson, 1905–.

Technical Book Review Index. Pittsburgh: Carnegie Library, 1917–29, 1935–.

YEARBOOKS, ALMANACS, AND HANDBOOKS

Annual Register of World Events: A Review of the Year. New York: St. Martin's, 1758–.

Dow Jones Irvin Business Almanac.

Facts on File. New York: Facts on File, 1940–.

Guinness Book of World Records. New York: Sterling, 1962.

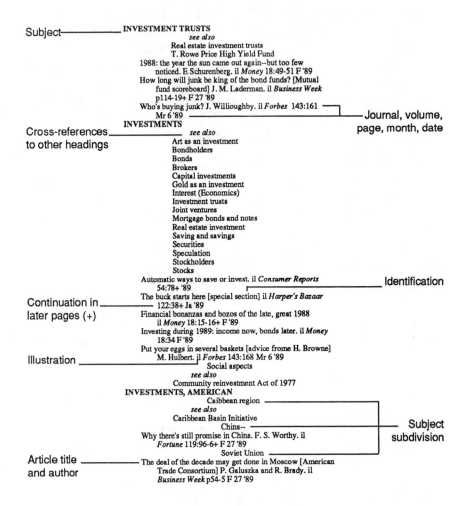

Subject —————— INVESTMENT TRUSTS
see also
Real estate investment trusts
T. Rowe Price High Yield Fund
1988: the year the sun came out again--but too few
noticed. E Schurenberg. il *Money* 18:49-51 F '89
How long will junk be king of the bond funds? [Mutual
fund scoreboard] J. M. Laderman. il *Business Week*
p114-19+ F 27 '89
Who's buying junk? J. Willioughby. il *Forbes* 143:161 —————— Journal, volume,
Mr 6 '89   page, month, date
Cross-references ————— INVESTMENTS
to other headings   *see also*
Art as an investment
Bondholders
Bonds
Brokers
Capital investments
Gold as an investment
Interest (Economics)
Investment trusts
Joint ventures
Mortgage bonds and notes
Real estate investment
Saving and savings
Securities
Speculation
Stockholders
Stocks
Automatic ways to save or invest. il *Consumer Reports* —————— Identification
54:78+ '89
Continuation in ————— The buck starts here [special section] il *Harper's Bazaar*
later pages (+)   122:38+ Ja '89
Financial bonanzas and bozos of the late, great 1988
il *Money* 18:15-16+ F '89
Investing during 1989: income now, bonds later. il *Money*
18:34 F '89
Put your eggs in several baskets [advice frome H. Browne]
Illustration ————— M. Hulbert. il *Forbes* 143:168 Mr 6 '89
Social aspects
see also
Community reinvestment Act of 1977
INVESTMENTS, AMERICAN
Caribbean region
see also
Caribbean Basin Initiative
China-- —————————————— Subject
Why there's still promise in China. F. S. Worthy. il   subdivision
Fortune 119:96-6+ F 27 '89
Soviet Union
Article title ————— The deal of the decade may get done in Moscow [American
and author   Trade Consortium] P. Galuszka and R. Brady. il
Business Week p54-5 F 27 '89

Figure 2:   Sample entries from *Readers' Guide to Periodical Literature*, April
10, 1989 edition, p. 85.

Subject ———— . RESORTS. Use Travel and Vacations ———
RESORTS INTERNATIONAL, INC. See also → ———— Cross-references
Gambling, Ap 1, My 12,19 ————
    Resorts International Inc directors reject Merv →
Griffin's revised takeover offer (S), Ap 5,IV,5;2
    Latest career of Merv Griffin, as corporate raider, is
getting off to slow start; Griffin engaged Donald Trump in
battle for Resorts International, hotel-casino chain, and offered
$36 a share for Resorts; so far, he has succeeded only in
derailing Trump's plan to take Resorts private; Resorts bid is
one of flurry of recent moves Griffin has made to escalate
building of his business empire; photos (M), Ap 9,I,37;3
    Griffin Co extends its offer to acquire Resorts
International Inc until 5 PM on April 18 (S), Ap 12,IV,3;5
    Merv Griffin, through his Griffin Co, will begin $36-
a-share tender offer for 51 percent of Resorts International (S) Length of article
Summary of   Inc's Class A shares (S), Ap 13,IV,4;3 ———— under colum
article ————— Donald J Trump, under pressure to agree to deal that
would benefit other shareholders of Resorts International Inc,
drops his opposition and agrees to sell his controlling interest
in Atlantic City, NJ, company to Merv Griffin; Trump, who is
expected to make profit of about $400 million, will retain
certain Resorts assets; photos; chronicle of deal (M), Ap
15,IV,1;4
    Donald J Trump's deal to sell his controlling interest
in Resorts International Inc to Merv Griffin collapses; proposed deal would have given Griffin control of Resorts casino
on the Boardwalk as well as real estate and casino operations
in Bahamas; Trump would have retained ownership of Taj
Date, section,   Mahal casino being built by Resorts in Atlantic City (M), My
page, column —12,IV,1;3

    Donald J Trump and Merv Griffin begin new talks on
giving Trump full control of Taj Mahal hotel and gambling
casino being built in Atlantic City and allowing Griffin to take
over Resorts International Inc (S), My 19,IV,5;2
    Donald J Trump and Merv Griffin say they have
again come to terms on plan to divide up assets of Resorts
International, ending two-week deadlock on secondary issues
that had threatened to destroy their deal (M) My 28,I33;6
    Resorts International approves agreement with Griffin
Co in which Resorts shareholders will receive $300 million
from Griffin for their shares (S), Je 28,I,39;2
    Merv Griffin begins tender offer for Class A shares of
Resorts International Inc (S), 8,IV,4;1

Figure 3: Sample entries from the *New York Times Quarterly Index*, April–
June, 1988.

Information Please Almanac. New York: Simon, 1947–.
Survey of Current Business.
The World Almanac and Book of Facts. New York: Newspaper En-
    terprise Assn., 1868–.

NEWSPAPER INDEXES

The biggest advantage of a newspaper index is the ability to locate
current information on a topic. Articles from back copies may be re-

Subject ————— **DOW JONES & CO., INC.**

Telerate Inc. and Intext Holdings Ltd. agreed to from an electronic trading system with the London International Financial Futures Exchange; Telerate is 67%-owned by Dow Jones & Co., Inc. 3/2-C15;4

Media stocks cath fire in wake of Time-Warner deal, but terms disappoint some Time shareholders (Heard on the Street) 3/7-C1;3

Summary of
article ————————— Two changes were made in the Dow Jones Equity Market Index as a result of the restructuring of Kaufman & Broad Inc.; a unit being spun off, Kaufman & Broad Home Corp., takes its former parent's place in the home-construction industry group; remaining portion of firm, which will change its name to Broad Inc., joins life-insurance industry group. 3/8-C6;4 ————————————— Identification

Gulf & Western shrugs off merger rumors, sees no pressure form Time-Warner proposal. (Heard on the Street) 3/14-C2;3

Hospital Corp of American was removed from the health-care providers group of the Dow Jones Equity Market Index, because firm was taken privatein a buy-out; Manor Care Inc. was added to the group 3/17-C6;2

William Kerby, former chairman and CEO of Dow Jones & Co. and one of the architects of the modern Wall Street Journal, died of cancer in Bethlehem, Pa.; he was 81 years old. 3/20-A6;3

Figure 4:   Sample entry from the *Wall Street Journal Index*, p. 23, March 1989, Dow Jones & Co.

searched using microfilm or microfiche files. For information on your topic, scan the various newspaper indexes at the beginning stage of research (see Figure 4).

THE CHICAGO TRIBUNE INDEX

CHRISTIAN SCIENCE MONITOR INDEX

THE NEW YORK TIMES INDEX

THE WALL STREET JOURNAL INDEX

THE WASHINGTON POST INDEX

3.5.2 Indexes of Business Subjects

BUSINESS PERIODICALS INDEX

The Business Periodicals Index contains information on all accounting, business, economics, and financial areas of study (see Figure 5).

Some other indexes useful to business researchers include:

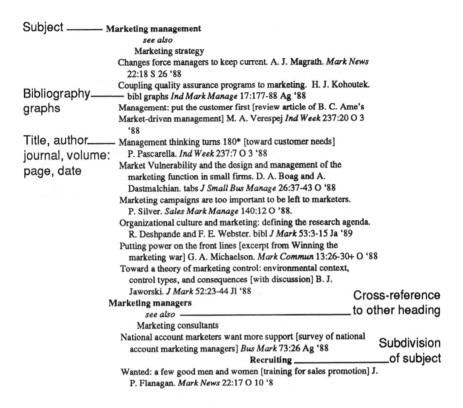

Subject ———— Marketing management
see also
Marketing strategy
Changes force managers to keep current. A. J. Magrath. *Mark News*
22:18 S 26 '88
Coupling quality assurance programs to marketing. H. J. Kohoutek.
Bibliography———— bibl graphs *Ind Mark Manage* 17:177-88 Ag '88
graphs   Management: put the customer first [review article of B. C. Ame's
Market-driven management] M. A. Verespej *Ind Week* 237:20 O 3
'88
Title, author———— Management thinking turns 180* [toward customer needs]
journal, volume: P. Pascarella. *Ind Week* 237:7 O 3 '88
page, date   Market Vulnerability and the design and management of the
marketing function in small firms. D. A. Boag and A.
Dastmalchian. tabs *J Small Bus Manage* 26:37-43 O '88
Marketing campaigns are too important to be left to marketers.
P. Silver. *Sales Mark Manage* 140:12 O '88.
Organizational culture and marketing: defining the research agenda.
R. Deshpande and F. E. Webster. bibl *J Mark* 53:3-15 Ja '89
Putting power on the front lines [excerpt from Winning the
marketing war] G. A. Michaelson. *Mark Commun* 13:26-30+ O '88
Toward a theory of marketing control: environmental context,
control types, and consequences [with discussion] B. J.
Jaworski. *J Mark* 52:23-44 Jl '88   Cross-reference
Marketing managers   to other heading
see also ——————————————————
Marketing consultants
National account marketers want more support [survey of national
account marketing managers] *Bus Mark* 73:26 Ag '88   Subdivision
Recruiting ——————————of subject
Wanted: a few good men and women [training for sales promotion] J.
P. Flanagan. *Mark News* 22:17 O 10 '8

Figure 5: Sample entries from *Business Periodicals Index*, April 1989, p. 491, Wilson Company, Inc., New York.

Accountant's Index, American Economic Association Index, Applied Science & Technology Index, Business Education Forum Index, Business Index, Business Periodicals Index, Business Publications Index and Abstracts, Computer Literature Index, Engineering Index, Environment Index, Hospitality Index, Insurance Index, Monthly Catalogue of United States Government Publication, Personnel Literature Index, Public Affairs Information Service Bulletin (PAIS), Social Sciences Citation Index, Social Science Index, U.S. Predicasts F & S Index.

3.5.3 Specialized Journals for Business Researchers

As a business major you will want to become familiar with as many specialized business publications as possible to help you locate information for your research topic. Listed below is a comprehensive compilation of many specialized business magazines and trade journals.

For example, if your area of interest is marketing, the journal *Target Marketing* reports current news stories dealing with direct marketing.

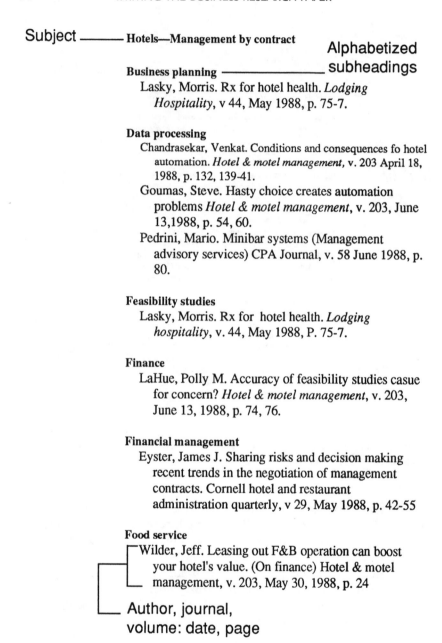

Subject ———— Hotels—Management by contract   Alphabetized

Business planning ————————— subheadings
> Lasky, Morris. Rx for hotel health. *Lodging Hospitality*, v 44, May 1988, p. 75-7.

Data processing
> Chandrasekar, Venkat. Conditions and consequences fo hotel automation. *Hotel & motel management,* v. 203 April 18, 1988, p. 132, 139-41.
> Goumas, Steve. Hasty choice creates automation problems *Hotel & motel management*, v. 203, June 13,1988, p. 54, 60.
> Pedrini, Mario. Minibar systems (Management advisory services) CPA Journal, v. 58 June 1988, p. 80.

Feasibility studies
> Lasky, Morris. Rx for hotel health. *Lodging hospitality*, v. 44, May 1988, P. 75-7.

Finance
> LaHue, Polly M. Accuracy of feasibility studies casue for concern? *Hotel & motel management*, v. 203, June 13, 1988, p. 74, 76.

Financial management
> Eyster, James J. Sharing risks and decision making recent trends in the negotiation of management contracts. Cornell hotel and restaurant administration quarterly, v 29, May 1988, p. 42-55

Food service
> Wilder, Jeff. Leasing out F&B operation can boost your hotel's value. (On finance) Hotel & motel management, v. 203, May 30, 1988, p. 24

Author, journal,
volume: date, page

Figure 6: Sample entries from *Accountant's Index*, 1988, p. 227.

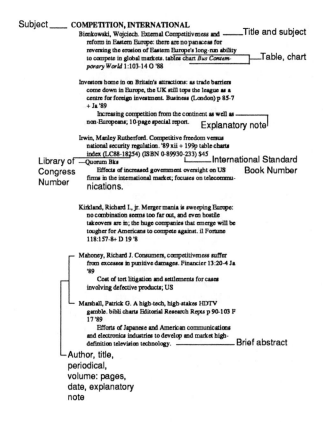

Figure 7: Sample entries from *Public Affairs Information Service Bulletin* (PAIS), March 1989, p. 83.

In the February 1989 issue, "What to Expect from a List Broker" and "Fueling the Phone Line" discuss the latest news on direct marketing.

ACCOUNTING:

Accountant, Accountants Digest, Accounting Review, CPA Journal, Internal Auditor, Journal of Accountancy, Journal of Accounting Research, Management Accounting, National Public Accountants, Practical Accountant, Price Waterhouse Review, Tax Practice Management, Taxation for Accountants, Woman CPA.

ADVERTISING:

Advertising Age, Advertising World, Adweek, Journal of Advertising, Broadcasting, Communication News, Editor and Publisher, International Journal of Advertising, Journal of Advertising, Journal of Advertising Research, Media Decisions, Public Relations Journal, Public Relations Review, Publishers Weekly, and Scan.

BUSINESS:

Beijing Review, Black Enterprise, Business Education, Business Horizons, Business Marketing, Business Month, Business Quarterly, Business Week, Canadian Business Review, Entrepreneurial Woman, Forbes, Fortune, Fortune Italia, Harvard Business Review, Journal of Business, Journal of Business Communications, Journal of Business Strategy, Journal of Contemporary Business, Journal of International Business, Journal of Small Business Management, Nation's Business, New England Business, Report on Business, Survey of Current Business, Venture, Wall Street Journal, and Working Woman.

BUSINESS EDUCATION:

Black Issues in Higher Education, Chronicle of Higher Education, College Teaching, Computing Teacher, Education and Computing, Education Digest, Education U.S.A., Education Week, Educational Leadership, Educational Research, Educational Studies, Educational Technology, Journal of Black Studies, Journal of Economic Education, Journal of Education for Business, Journal of Educational Computing Research, Journal of Educational Research, Journal of Educational Technology Systems, Journal of Higher Education, Journal of Nutrition Education, National Association for Business Teacher Education Review, Peabody Journal of Education, Teacher's College Record, and Technology Teacher.

CULINARY ARTS:

Alcohol Health & Research World, Bakery Production & Marketing, Baking, Bon Appetit, Chocolatier, Cooking for Profit, Cooks Magazine, Culinarian: The Official Publication of Chefs Association of The Pacific Coast, Dairy & Food Sanitation, Dairy Foods, Food & Nutrition Bulletin, Food & Wine, Food Engineering, Food Management, Food Production Management, Food Technology, Foodservice Equipment & Supplies Specialists, Foodservice Product News, Friends of Wine, Frozen Food Digest, Gourmet, Journal of Food Safety, Journal Gastronomy, Meat & Poultry, Meat Source, Nutrition Action Health Letter, Packer, Poultry Times. Prepared Foods, Seafood Leader, Wine Country, and Vintage: The Consumer Magazine For Wine, Beer, Spirits & Cheese.

DATA PROCESSING:

Byte, Computer, Computer Business News, Computer Communications Decisions, Computer + Electronics, Computer Data, Computer Decisions, Computer Digest, Computer Industry Report, Computer Law Journal, Computer Pictures, Computers and People, Computer Security Journal, Computer Weekly, Computerworld, Data Communications, Data Management, Datamation, Desktop Computing, IBM Journal of Research and Development, I.E.E.E. Computer Magazine,

Information and Records Management, Infosystems, Information Systems News, Macworld, Micro, Microcomputing, Mini-Micro Systems, Nibble, P.C. Magazine, P.C. Tech Journal, P.C. Week, PC World, Personal Computing, Small Business Computers, Software News, and Word Processing World.

ECONOMICS:

Akron Business and Economic Review, American Economic Review, American Economist, Applied Economics, Business Economics, Economic Record, The Economist, Far-Eastern Economic Review, Journal of Economic Issues, Journal of Economics & Business, Journal of Labor Economics, Journal of Political Economy, Journal of Urban Economics, Land Economics, Rand Journal of Economics, Review of Economics and Statistics, and Review of Black Political Economy.

FINANCE:

American Banker, Bank of Canada Review, The Banker, Bankers Magazine, Bankers Monthly, Banking, Banking Journal, Barron's, Business Credit, Credit and Banking, Commercial Financing, Euromoney, Finance, Finance and Development, Financial Analysts Journal, Financial Digest, Financial Executive, Financial Management, Financial Times Newspaper, Financial World, Forbes, Governmental Finance, Journal of Money, Journal of Money, Credit, and Banking, Mergers and Acquisitions, Money, Mortgage Banker, and Pension World.

HOSPITALITY:

Cooking For Profit, Cornell Hotel and Restaurant Administration Quarterly, Food Management, Food-service Equipment & Supplies Specialist, Hotel/Motel Security Safety Management, Hotel and Motel Management, Hotel and Restaurant International, Hotel Resort Industry, Hotel Sales and Marketing Review, International Journal of Hospitality Management, Journal of Foodservice Systems, Journal of Leisure Research, Journal of Time Research, Lodging, Lodging Hospitality, Meetings and Conventions, Meeting News, Military Clubs and Recreation, Nation's Restaurant News, Resort Development, Restaurant/Hotel Design International, Restaurants & Institutions, Restaurant Business, Restaurant Hospitality, Restaurant Management, Restaurant USA, School Foodservice Journal, Successful Meetings, and Tourism.

MANAGEMENT:

Academy of Management Journal, Across the Board, Administrative Management, Administrative Science Quarterly, Advanced Management Journal, Business Horizons, Business Month, Business Week, California Management Review, Canadian Manager, Entrepreneurship: Theory and Practice, International Management, Journal of Applied Management, Journal of General Management, Management In-

ternational Review, Management Research, Management Review, Management Science, Management Today, Management World, Organizational Dynamics, Personnel Journal, Personnel Management, Research Management, Sloan Management Review, and Supervisory Management.

MARKETING:

Business Marketing, Chain Merchandiser Magazine, Direct Marketing, Distribution, Distribution Worldwide, Incentive Marketing, Industrial Distribution, Industrial Marketing, Industrial Marketing Management, Journal of Marketing, Journal of Marketing Research, Mainly Marketing, Marketing Communication, Marketing and Media Decisions, Marketing News, Marketing Times, Product Marketing, Purchasing, and Target Marketing.

OFFICE MANAGEMENT:

Administrative Management: The Magazine of Office and Automation, Human Resources Management, Journal of Technical Writing and Communication, Modern Office Procedures, Modern Office Technology, National Shorthand, The Office, The Office Professional, Personnel Journal, Professional Medical Assistant, Public Administration Review, Public Personnel Management, Reporter, Secretary, Supervisory Management, Today's Office, and The Writer.

RETAILING:

American Fabrics and Fashion, Chain Store Age, Computer Retailing News, Discount Merchandiser, Harper's Bazaar, Harper's Magazine, Journal of Retailing, Purchasing, Retail Control, Sales and Marketing Digest, Textile World, Stores, Store Design, Textile World, Vogue, and Visual Merchandising & Store Design.

3.5.4 Additional Specialized Business References

The following are additional references for the business researcher.

1. American Economic Business History: Information Sources. *R.W. Lovett, ed. Detroit: Gale, 1971.*
2. *Area Wage Surveys.* U.S. Bureau of Labor Statistics. Washington, DC: Government Printing Office, 1950–.
3. *Barron's.* New York: Dow Jones, 1921–.
4. *Barron's Finance and Investment Handbook.* Woodbury, N.Y.: Barron's Educational Series, 1986.
5. *Black's Law Dictionary.* Henry Campbell Black. 5th ed. St. Paul MN: West Publishing, 1979.
6. *Business Information: How to Find It, How to Use It.* Michael R. Lavin. Phoenix, AZ: Oryx Press, 1987.
7. *Business Information Sources.* Lorna M. Daniells. Berkeley, CA: University of California Press, 1985.
8. *Business Organizations and Agencies Directory.* Anthony T. Kruzas, Robert C. Thomas, and Kay Gill, eds. Detroit, MI: Gale 1986.

9. *Business Software Directory.* Ruth K. Koolish, ed. Glenview, IL: Information Sources, Inc., 1986.
10. *Business Statistics.* U.S. Department of Commerce. Washington, DC: Government Printing Office. 1932–.
11. *Computer Dictionary.* Charles J. Sippl. 4th ed. New York: Howard Sams & Co., 1985.
12. *Consultants and Consulting Organizations Directory.* Janice McLean, ed. 7th ed. Detroit, MI: Gale, 1986.
13. *Corporate Technology Directory.* Wellesley Hills, MA: Corp Tech, 1986.
14. *CRB Commodity Yearbook.* New York: Commodity Research Bureau. 1939–.
15. *Dictionary for Accountants.* Eric L. Kohler. 5th ed. Englewood Cliffs: Prentice, 1975.
16. *Directory of Foreign Firms Operating in the U.S.* 5th ed. New York: Uniworld Business Publications, 1986.
17. *Directory of Management Consultants.* 4th ed. Fitzwilliam, NH: Consultants News, 1986.
18. *Directory of Online Databases.* New York: Cuadra/Elsevier.
19. *Directory of United States Importers.* New York: Journal of Commerce.
20. *Employment and Earnings.* U.S. Bureau of Labor Statistics. Washington, DC: Government Printing Office, 1909–.
21. *Encyclopedia of Associations.* Katherine Gruber, ed. 21st ed. Detroit, MI: Gale, 1987.
22. *Encyclopedia of Banking and Finance.* Glenn G. Munn and Ferdinand L. Garcia. 8th ed. Boston: Bankers Publishing, 1984.
23. *Encyclopedia of Business Information Sources.* James Woy, ed. 6th ed. Detroit, MI: Gale, 1986.
24. *Encyclopedia of Economics.* Douglas Greenwald, ed. New York: McGraw-Hill, 1982.
25. *Encyclopedia of Information Systems and Services.* Amy Lucas, ed. 7th ed. Detroit, MI: Gale, 1987.
26. *Encyclopedia of International Commerce.* William J. Miller. Centreville, MD: Cornell Maritime Press, 1985.
27. *Encyclopedia of Management.* Carl Heyel, ed. 3rd ed. New York: Van Nostrand, 1983.
28. *Europa Year Book: A World Survey.* Detroit, MI: Gale, 1926–.
29. *Exporter's Directory/U.S. Buying Guide.* New York: Journal of Commerce.
30. *Exporter's Encyclopedia.* New York: Dun & Bradstreet.
31. *Facts on File Dictionary of Personnel Management and Labor Relations.* Jay Shafritz. 2nd ed. Revised and expanded. New York: Facts on File, 1985.
32. *Fairchild's Financial Manual of Retail Stores.* New York: Fairchild Publications.
33. *Handbook of the Bond and Money Markets.* David M. Darst. New York: McGraw-Hill, 1981.
34. *Handbook of Corporate Finance.* Edward I. Altman, ed. New York: Wiley, 1986.
35. *Handbook of Financial Markets and Institutions.* Edward I. Altman, ed. New York: Wiley, 1987.
36. *Handbook of Human Resources Administration.* Joseph J. Famularo, ed. 2nd ed. New York: McGraw-Hill, 1986.

37. *Handbook of International Business.* Ingo Walter and Tracy Murray, eds. New York: Wiley, 1982.
38. *Handbook of International Financial Management.* Allen Sweeney and Robert Rachlins, eds. New York: McGraw-Hill, 1984.
39. *Handbook of Modern Accounting.* Sidney Davidson and Roman Will. 3rd ed. New York: McGraw-Hill, 1983.
40. *Handbook of Modern Marketing.* Victor P. Buell, ed. 2nd. New York: McGraw-Hill, 1986.
41. *International Dictionary of Business.* Hano Johannsen and G. Terry Page. Englewood Cliffs: Prentice, 1981.
42. *Investors Encyclopedia.* Chet Currier. New York: Franklin Watts, 1985.
43. *Kohler's Dictionary for Accountants.* W. W. Cooper and Yuii Ijiri, eds. 6th ed. Englewood Cliffs, NJ: Prentice-Hall, 1983.
44. *The Language of Real Estate.* John W. Reilly. 2nd ed. New York: Real Estate Education, 1982.
45. *The Language of Wall Street.* Peter Wyckoff. New York: Hopkinson, 1973.
46. *Lesly's Public Relations Handbook.* Philip Lesly. 3rd ed. Englewood Cliffs, NJ: Prentice-Hall, 1983.
47. *Letitia Baldridge's Complete Guide to Executive Manners.* New York: Rawson Associates, 1985.
48. *MacRae's State Industrial Directories.* New York: State Manufacturing Directories, 1959–.
49. *McGraw-Hill Dictionary of Modern Economics.* Douglas Greenwald, et al. 3rd ed. New York: McGraw-Hill, 1983.
50. *Marconi's International Register.* New York: Telegraphic Cable and Radio Registrations, 1898–.
51. *No-Load Mutual Fund Guide.* William E. Donoghue and Thomas Tilling. New York: Bantam, 1984.
52. *Oxbridge Directory of Newsletters.* Matthew Manning, ed. New York: Oxbridge Communications.
53. *Paine-Weber Handbook of Stocks and Bond Analysis.* Kiril Sokoloff. New York: McGraw-Hill, 1979.
54. *Polk's World Bank Directory.* Nashville, TN: Polk and Co., 1895–.
55. *Prentice-Hall Dictionary of Business, Finance and Law.* Michael Downey Rice. Englewood Cliffs, NJ: Prentice-Hall, 1983.
56. *Production Handbook.* John A. White, ed. 4th ed. New York: Wiley, 1986.
57. *Questions and Answers on Real Estate.* Robert W. Semenow. 9th ed. Englewood Cliffs, NJ: Prentice-Hall, 1979.
58. *Real Estate Law.* Robert Kratovil and Raymond J. Werner. 9th ed. Englewood Cliffs, NJ: Prentice-Hall, 1983.
59. *Sales and Marketing Management.* New York: Bill Communications, 1918–.
60. *Small Business Sourcebook.* Robert J. Elster. 2nd ed. Detroit, MI: Gale, 1986.
61. *Successful Investing: A Complete Guide to Your Financial Future.* United Business Service Co. New York: Simon & Schuster, 1987.
62. *Television and Cable Factbook.* Washington, DC: Television Digest, 1982– .
63. *Thomas' Register of American Manufactures.* New York: Thomas Publishing, 1905–.

64. *Thorndike Encyclopedia of Banking and Financial Tables.* Boston: Warren, Gorham, and Lamont, 1980–.
65. *Trade Names Dictionary.* Donna Wood, ed. 5th ed. Detroit, MI: Gale.
66. *Trade Shows and Professional Exhibits Directory.* Robert J. Elster, ed. 2nd ed. Detroit, MI: Gale, 1987.
67. *Ulrich's International Periodicals Directory.* New York: Bowker, 1932–.
68. *Value Line Investment Survey.* New York: Arnold Bernard 1937–.
69. *The VNR Investor's Dictionary.* New York: Van Nostrand Reinhold, 1980.
70. *Ward's Business Directory.* Belmont, CA: Information Access Company.

3.6 INFOTRAC

Infotrac is a computerized reference system that allows the researcher to retrieve bibliographical references for newspapers and magazines stored on compact disc. Some databases available on the Infotrac system include The Academic Index, General Periodicals Index, Government Publications Index, The Magazine Index/Plus, and National Newspaper Index. This new technology makes searching references for a topic faster and easier than scanning printed indexes. If it is available in your library, by all means use it.

The subject headings in Infotrac are organized alphabetically according to author, title, or subject. Suppose you want to find an article about achievements of women in business. First, type in the topic "Women in Business," then press the SEARCH/ENTER key. The screen will display a full listing of topic headings and subheadings for women in business. Next position the cursor next to the subject heading you have chosen, (Achievements and Awards) and press SEARCH/ENTER key. A citations window will appear on the screen and display the bibliographical references for your topic of research. Press the PRINT key, and the printer will print out a complete bibliographical reference, with title of article, author, publication information, and page numbers of article.

You do not need to write out the citations because the printer does it for you, quickly and accurately. This system saves you time and makes the search easier.

Sample Citation

WOMEN IN BUSINESS
–achievements and awards

Beating the odds, (women business owners) by Nancy Croft Baker il   v76   Nation's Business   Sept '88   p40(2)
46B0297   40P1452

Georgia Cashman. (Top Ten Business Women of ABWA) il   v41   Women in Business   March-April '89   p49(1)

Beating the odds, (women business owners) by Nancy Croft Baker il   v76   Nation's Business   Sept '88   p40(2)
46B0297   40P1452

Sonia Jones: once a humble PhD in Spanish, she's now the yogurt queen of Nova Scotia. (The Successors) by Harry Bruce il   v61   Canadian Business   Aug '88   p56(2)
45M2404   39Y2441

Entrepreneurs of the year; Indiana Business present profiles of the eight winners of the Entrepreneur of the Year Awards. by Melinda Church il   v32   Indiana Business Magazine   Aug '88   p14(5)
41T0358

Jean Hollis. (successful women profiles) il   v40   Women in Business   July-Aug '88   p35(2)

Profiles of success. (three of top ten business women of American Business Women's Association) il   v39   Women in Business   July-Aug '87   p32(4)

Independents win 1986 Pacesetter Awards. (restaurant awards to women) il   v48   Independent Restaurants   Sept '86   p62(2)
26T2956

Application Activities

1. Make a get acquainted visit to your library. In your researcher's notebook indicate the answers to the following questions:

   a. What is the name of a librarian who answers business/economic questions and helps with research in these areas?

   b. Does your library use the Dewey Decimal system or the Library of Congress system, or both?

   c. What is the procedure for using books on reserve and checking out books?

   d. What are the opening and closing hours weekdays and weekends? Is the library open holidays, Sundays, and intersessions?

   e. Are catalog cards filed separately by author, title, and subject, or all together in alphabetical order?

   f. Is there computerized access to materials owned by your library?

   g. For how long may books be checked out? Is there a fine for overdue books?

2. Visit the reference room and find as many of the following sources that your library has. Write down the call number and/or location of each of the following:

   Reader's Guide to Periodical Literature
   PAIS Bulletin
   Applied Science and Technology Index
   New York Times Index
   Biography Index
   Business Index
   Business Periodicals Index
   Accountants Index
   Encyclopedia Britannica

3.

338.0973	The economic transformation of America Heilbroner, Robert L. The economic transformation of America / Robert L. Heilbroner, in collaboration with Aaron Singer. --New York : Harcourt Brace Jovanovich, c1977. xi, 276 p. : ill. ; 21 cm. Bibliography: p. 254-258. Includes index. ISBN 0-15-518800-3 1. United States--Economic conditions 2. United States--Industries--History. I. Singer, Aaron, Joint author. II. Title HC103.h39 2811690 338.0373 76-24990

    a. Is this an author card, title card, or subject card?
    b. Who published this book?
    c. What is the call number?
    d. Under what subjects is this book listed?

4. What information does your card catalog or computer catalog give you about two of the following books:

    a. *The Great Depression of 1990* by Batra Ravi.

    b. *What's Ahead for the Economy: The Challenge and the Chance* by Louis Rukeyser.

    c. *Re-Inventing the Corporation: Transforming Your Job and Your Company for the New Information Society* by John Naisbitt and Patricia Aberdeen.

5. ACCOUNTANT'S INDEX

In any quarterly issue of the *Accountant's Index*, how many entries are listed under the heading "Computer Security" or "White Collar Crime?" Write out the periodical title, volume, and date for an article on one of these topics.

6. WALL STREET JOURNAL INDEX

In a monthly issue of the Wall Street Journal (WSJ) Index, Eastern Edition, locate a company name. Write out the full entry for one abstract under that heading. Look up any topic in the general news section of the same WSJ index. Using the key in the front of the index translate the elements for both entries.

7. NEW YORK TIMES INDEX

In the 1987 *New York Times Index* Proctor & Gamble names L. Ross Love and Robert L. Wehling newly appointed managers to the company. What is the date, section, page, and column, of the story's publication? Use the key at the front of the Index to help you.

8. INFOTRAC (if applicable)

   Locate an INFOTRAC terminal in your library. Read the user's instructions before you begin. Assume that you want to locate articles on the topic "Marketing." Press SEARCH/ENTER to start INFOTRAC. Type in MARKETING. How many citations are listed? Read each citation. Using the prior-line key, scroll back to and print citations #5, #9, #10, and #14. Read each printed citation. What information is given by each citation?

4

CONDUCTING
A DATABASE
SEARCH

Learning Objectives

Upon completing this chapter you should be able to:

1. Explain the advantages and disadvantages of online data base searches.
2. Explain the steps necessary to conduct a database search.
3. Differentiate between online and offline database searches.
4. Use both print and electronic research techniques.

4.1 ONLINE INFORMATION SERVICES

Two developments—the rate at which man is generating new knowledge and the revolution in computer technology—have enhanced the manner in which research is conducted. For one thing, the information explosion has been so rapid that it is no longer possible for traditional methods of indexing information (printed or "hardcopy" sources) to keep pace with the flood of information. In addition, it has always been a practice of libraries to provide access to information and materials beyond the scope of their collections, a worthy goal but one difficult to achieve. To help student researchers cope with these new realities, online database systems enable students to tap into business information from outside sources.

At present, most database searches are used by graduate students and business professionals who require up-to-date information not yet in conventional library sources. It seems inevitable, however, that before long, database searching will be the most efficient way for all researchers to keep abreast of the very latest business information. The skilled researcher then, should not only have mastered the search techniques discussed in Chapter 3, but must also be able to access the new technology. Bear in mind, however, that mastery of traditional research methods is a necessary prerequisite to database searching.

Advantages of Online Database Searches

1. Online searches are faster and more efficient.
   a. By using more than one subject term simultaneously, online searching can refine search results much more precisely and quickly than most manual searches.
   b. Access to information is better. Not only can subjects be searched, but even article and book titles and abstracts (summaries) can be scanned for relevant words and phrases.
2. Online searches can locate the most recent information, even some items that a library may not yet have received and others not published except in machine-readable (computerized) format.
3. Searching several online systems may quickly provide a broad scan of all available data.

Disadvantages of Online Database Searches

1. Some libraries may not yet have this new technology available.
2. If available, access for researchers may be limited by time and competing demands to use the systems.
3. The researcher most likely will have to pay for the telecommunication service, the database service, and/or the amount of time it takes for the computer to perform the search. It is worth asking if the library or the university will cover any part of the cost.
4. For some topics a database search must be supplemented by a manual search (e.g., where information sources are not covered by online vendors or where specific terminology for new topics is not yet well-defined).

4.2 HOW A DATABASE SEARCH IS MADE

An online database searches for information via a telecommunication link, a terminal, a keyboard, a monitor, a printer, and a telephone hookup known as a modem. When you perform an online database search, you are tapping into databases located throughout the country, and in a short period you can electronically retrieve an abundance of data that would take weeks to collect manually looking though traditional printed sources. Researchers who perform a database search can locate precise business and financial information such as financial reports, market research, government statistics, reports to stockholders, banking news, and much more.

4.2.1 The Specialized Search Librarian

One option for tapping into this wealth of information is using the expertise of a specialized librarian who is trained to use the various systems. The librarian will understand the technical information of the database systems, as well as the many specialized codes and preferred search terms used by different databases. These are the signals which tell the computer to locate the information you need.

Once you decide that you want to use a computer service to help you write a paper, make an appointment with the search specialist in the library. The specialist will identify the charges involved and determine whether the service is appropriate for your project. If you decide to use the service, at some point you will be asked to go through the following steps:

1. Identify the field (e.g., accounting, management, computers) you wish to research. The specialized librarian will help you choose the best database(s) for your field of research.
2. Provide a one- or two-sentence narrative description of the topic to search, and define phrases with special meaning.
3. List logical operators or closely related descriptors to help define your ideas.
4. If possible, give names of a few journals that might be central to your search and/or any key authors or articles you have already found.

The basis of a search is identifying information sources (books, journals, statistical reports) to match specific topics, places, or names. For example, if you wish to learn more about the subject "employment as it relates to minority groups and earnings," you must identify the concepts that are part of the idea, issue, or phenomenon you will be researching. The specialized librarian will use these concepts to recommend a database(s) for the information you want on the subject of minorities and wages. For this example, the key concepts are MINORITIES AND EMPLOYMENT and DISCRIMINATION. Next, decide how these logical operators will relate to your purposes and frame a research question: How does discrimination reduce minority employment? The combination of these three concepts will control the search for citations dealing with the topic of discrimination and employment and eliminate most unrelated bibliographic references. Finally, your ideas must be translated into descriptors or subject terms used to classify information in whatever database you intend to use.

Search strategy (logic) determines how broad or narrow the retrieved results will be. This is accomplished by using different combinations of AND, OR, or NOT. Examples might read (see Figures 8 and 9):

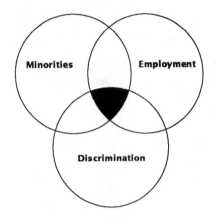

Figure 8:   Combination of concepts.

Search Request Form   DIALOG

Information Services, Inc.

TO BE FILLED OUT BY REQUESTOR

Requestor Name: *Jane Doe*

Address: *Central University*   Date: *Jan 19 —*

Telephone: _____

Search Title: _____

Narrative Description of Topic: *To determine whether discrimination against minorities exists in the workplace*

Date Required: *Feb 15 —*

Known Authors or Articles: _____

Types of Materials of Interest: All ____ If not "All", specify as follows:
Articles __X__ Reports _____ Patents _____ Conference Papers _____
Books _____ Dissertations _____ Other _____

Year to be Covered (only if such a limit is necessary) *1987-88*

Languages of Interest: All _____
If not "All", specify those of interest: *English*

How many relevant items do you think might be found?: _____

Maximum amount to be spent: _____

TO BE FILLED OUT BY SEARCHER

Formats to be used: _____

Results to be done: TYPEd _____ PRINTed _____

Preliminary databases to consider: _____

Appointment scheduled for: (time) _____

Searcher Name _____ Date _____

320003-002

Figure 9:   Dialog forms.

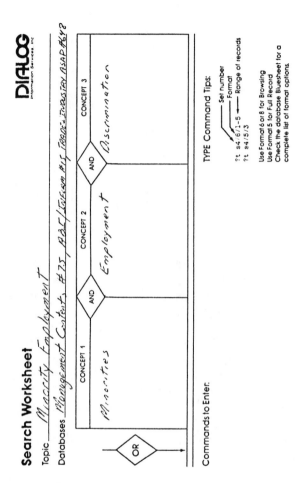

Search Worksheet

Topic: *Minority Employment*

Databases: *Management Contents #75, ABI/Inform #15, Trade-Industry ASAP #648*

CONCEPT 1 — *Minorities*

CONCEPT 2 — *Employment*

CONCEPT 3 — *Discrimination*

OR

AND

AND

Commands to Enter:

TYPE Command Tips:
- Set number
- Format
- Range of records

?t s4/6/1-5
?t s4/5/3

Use Format 6 or 8 for Browsing
Use Format 5 for Full Record
Check the database Bluesheet for a
complete list of format options.

Figure 9: *continued*

MINORITIES **AND** EMPLOYMENT **AND** DISCRIMINATION
MINORITIES **AND** (DISCRIMINATION **OR** PREJUDICE) **AND**
EMPLOYMENT
MINORITIES (**NOT** WOMEN) **AND** DISCRIMINATION **AND**
EMPLOYMENT

The computer will search through databases to select only articles
that match the darkened area because those articles contain all three
key concepts. In this example the specialized librarian has selected
MANAGEMENT CONTENTS, FILE 75, to conduct the search through
DIALOG information services.

RESEARCH QUESTION: How does discrimination reduce mi-
                            nority employment?

SEARCH TERMS: Minorities AND Employment AND
                            Discrimination.

PUBLICATION DATES:	1987–1988
FIND:	Minorities AND Employment AND Discrimination.

1364	MINORITIES
8833	EMPLOYMENT
2717	DISCRIMINATION
14859	PY = 1987 : PY = 1988*
9	MINORITIES AND EMPLOY-MENT AND DISCRIMINATION/ 1987:1988

* PY stands for Public Year.

You can see from the results of this search that there are 1,364 references matched with MINORITIES, 8,833 references matched with EMPLOYMENT, and 2,717 references matched with DISCRIMINA-TION, but only nine references matched with all three search words and published in 1987 or 1988.

Once you have determined your search strategy, the specialized librarian turns on the equipment and enters your search terms into the computer. The modem continuously transmits the message from the search terminal over telephone lines to a larger computer at a remote location via a telecommunications service such as Telenet or Tymnet while the search librarian interacts with the computer, keyboard, monitor, and printer.

The data found in most DIALOG databases fall into one of the following categories:

BIBLIOGRAPHIC RECORDS—contain citations (basic bibliographic references) with authors, titles, original source information, and often, an abstract (brief summary) of the article.

COMPLETE TEXT RECORD—contains full narrative text of a journal article, book, or newspaper.

DIRECTORIES—contain full record of directories, dictionaries and handbooks, companies, associations, and famous people. This may include addresses, phone numbers, product description, and annual sales for a company.

NUMERIC DATA—contain records of numeric statistics, tables, and financial data.

Dialog Bibliographic Record

Database number

Vendor

File name

Article title

Author

Journal

Month

Year

Volume

Length

0372494   DIALOG Information Services, File 75:   Management Contents
Student recruitment in black and white. (recruitment of minority
accounting students in Great Britain)
Sharp, Kenneth
Accountancy   v100   Aug, 1987, p.15(2)
SOURCE FILE: MC File 75

0371471 DIALOG Information Services, File 75:   Management Contents
Discrimination, human capital, and black-white unemployment: evidence
from cities.
Shulman, Steven
Journal of Human Resources v22 Summ, 1987,   p361(16)
SOURCE FILE: MC File 75

0366335 DIALOG Information Services, File 75:   Management Contents
An EEO-AA program that exceeds quotas - it targets biases. (equal employment
opportunity and affirmative action)
Poole, Jeanne C.; Kautz, E. Theodore
Personnel Journal v66 Jan, 1987,   p103(3)

4.3 COMPUTERIZED DATABASE SEARCHES

4.3.1 Dialog Information Service

Of all the online systems, DIALOG has the largest number of databases covering business, economics, and the social sciences. The databases on the DIALOG system contain more than 175 million records or units of information. For the business researcher, Foreigner Traders Index, Moody's Corporate News, Findex, BioBusiness, Management Contents, ABI/Inform, Business Dateline, Japan Economic Newswire Plus, and Computer Database are just some of the most relevant databases that are available.

4.3.2 Other Online Services

In addition to using DIALOG INFORMATION SERVICE, some university libraries are using BRS (BIBLIOGRAPHIC RETRIEVAL SERV-

ICE). Both offer reduced rates in the evening or on weekend. BRS AFTER DARK and DIALOG'S KNOWLEDGE INDEX are online all night to offer service at a reduced rate. The INFORMATION BANK is a current affairs database which retrieves articles and abstracts published in the New York Times and other database publications. Some other computer search services useful to the business researcher include THE SOURCE, COMPUSERVE, LEXIS (LAW), AND NEXIS (NEWS AND PUBLIC AFFAIRS). These can be used via a home or office terminal with a suitable phone hookup.

Dialog Bibliographic Record and Abstract

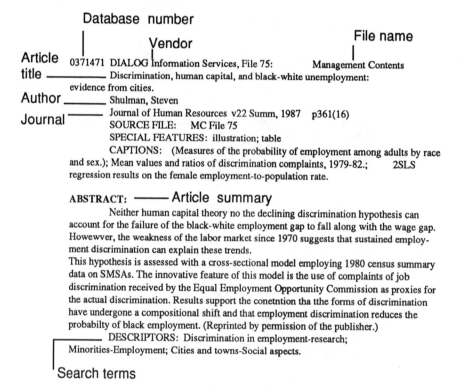

Database number

Vendor   File name

Article   0371471   DIALOG Information Services, File 75:   Management Contents
title ————————— Discrimination, human capital, and black-white unemployment:
      evidence from cities.
Author ———————— Shulman, Steven
Journal ———— Journal of Human Resources v22 Summ, 1987   p361(16)
          SOURCE FILE: MC File 75
          SPECIAL FEATURES: illustration; table
          CAPTIONS: (Measures of the probability of employment among adults by race
and sex.); Mean values and ratios of discrimination complaints, 1979-82.;   2SLS
regression results on the female employment-to-population rate.

ABSTRACT: ———— Article summary
        Neither human capital theory no the declining discrimination hypothesis can
account for the failure of the black-white employment gap to fall along with the wage gap.
Howevver, the weakness of the labor market since 1970 suggests that sustained employment discrimination can explain these trends.
This hypothesis is assessed with a cross-sectional model employing 1980 census summary
data on SMSAs. The innovative feature of this model is the use of complaints of job
discrimination received by the Equal Employment Opportunity Commission as proxies for
the actual discrimination. Results support the conetntion tha tthe forms of discrimination
have undergone a compositional shift and that employment discrimination reduces the
probabilty of black employment. (Reprinted by permission of the publisher.)
         ———— DESCRIPTORS: Discrimination in employment-research;
      Minorities-Employment; Cities and towns-Social aspects.

Search terms

4.3.3 Offline Searches—Compact Disc Reference Sources

Some university libraries offer offline search services to students, faculty, and professional users. The researcher can search offline (not through the telephone line) usually without the expense of search time and without the help of a specialized librarian. ABI/Inform and Business Periodicals on Disk are examples of the rapidly growing number of compact disc reference sources that hold business information. Business researchers can rely on compact disc references for answers to questions about companies, products, business conditions, corporate strategies, and management policies. This service allows the user to locate the latest business information with the option of printing abstracts and/or full texts of the journal article. Business subjects covered in ABI/Inform Compact Disc include: accounting and auditing, banking, data processing and information management, marketing, advertising and sales management, new product development, personnel, real estate, and telecommunications.

Conducting an offline database search is similar to online searches in that preparation and planning are required. As before, you must trigger the system by choosing key terms that narrow the scope of your search. For example, if you wish to learn how industry provides child care benefits to employees as part of fringe benefit packages, your search words might be: INDUSTRY—EMPLOYEE BENEFITS—CHILD CARE. In this case, the search would uncover articles with author, journal, publication information, search terms, and abstract.

ABI/INFORM

Title:	Dabbling with Diversity
Authors:	Malovaney, Dan
Journal:	Executive Financial Woman Vol: 1 Iss: 3 Date: Mar/Apr 1986 pp: 22–26 Jrnl Code: EFW
Terms:	Banking industry; Financial institutions; Employee benefits; Child care; Fringe benefits; Cafeteria plans (PER); Flexible
Codes:	8100 (Financial services industry); 6400 (Employee benefits & compensation)

Abstract: Banks are among the trendsetting corporations that are beginning to provide child care programs as part of their benefit packages. The changing lifestyle of the workforce has brought about reform of executive compensation. In the past 2 years, the number of corporations providing some form of child care as part of their benefits has increased from 1,000 to 2,500. In many cases, child care is included in a flexible benefit program that permits employees to pick their benefits, which might also include catastrophic medical and life insurance. Because only 15% of all employees are in the child-bearing or child-raising age group, flexible compensation provides a creative solution to the issue of equitability. From the employer's point of view, child care benefits can also benefit the company through less tardiness, better attitudes, and even good public relations.

Libraries subscribe to monthly updating, which keeps offline searches from being quite as current as online searches. There can be a small charge for using such compact disc services.

4.4 USING BOTH RESEARCH METHODS

As you have learned, research methods have changed and undoubtedly will continue to change. It is tempting to the student researcher to abandon the older methods in favor of the new technology. After all, database searching is unquestionably faster and more efficient than poring through stacks of books and journals and often faster than using printed indexes. Why not be completely modern?

The answer is, of course, that while you need to learn to use database searches, it does not necessarily follow that older research methods have to be set aside. They should not. One should complement the other. Manual searching still has many advantages for the student researcher, not the least of which is that it is almost always less expensive. Further, not all information is covered by computerized databases. And some topics can be done online but not in a cost-effectve manner. Finally, browsing through a library is still one of the most enjoyable intellectual acts, an act that almost always uncovers valuable unanticipated resources. It is in your own self-interest then, as we move towards the twenty-first century, to master techniques of traditional researching first and then, with a bow to progress, avail yourself of the wonders of today's database searches.

Application Activities

1. Find out what database services your college library offers.
    a. Does your library offer database reference services to its students? Are there restrictions for undergraduates? Graduate students?
    b. Is there a specialized librarian to conduct searches for undergraduate or graduate students?
    c. How much does your library charge for a database search?
2. Select one of the DIALOG databases in section 4.3 of this chapter that you think would be helpful for your research paper.
    a. Write a short narrative about what you wish to find out from that database.
    b. Write a research question for your topic.
    c. Identify the three main components or concepts for your search question.
3. Assume that you want to prepare a database search for each situation listed below. Write three possible search terms for each situation.

a. To locate articles on the growth of the hotel industry in the United States.

b. To locate articles on how advertisers depict women in their ads.

c. To locate articles on the decline of U.S. dominance in the global market.

4. Using the connecting words OR, AND, or NOT, show how a different combination of the terms in question number three could make your topic broader or narrower in scope.

5

OBTAINING PRIMARY INFORMATION

Learning Objectives

Upon completing this chapter you should be able to:

1. Distinguish between primary and secondary research.
2. Develop a questionnaire following the ten principles of survey question design.
3. Prepare and administer mail surveys, telephone surveys, and in-person surveys.
4. Conduct personal interviews and other field research techniques.
5. Analyze and evaluate primary information.

5.1 DEFINING PRIMARY RESEARCH

Most business research papers have as their starting point the library resources discussed in chapters 3 and 4. It makes good sense to begin your search by discovering what has already been done in your field of inquiry. For our purposes, we classify this activity as "secondary" research, that is, the searching for information already in print. This gathering of data from various business publications may be all that is needed to satisfy the requirements of most research assignments, but it is not the sole method of doing so.

Many assignments require that you move outside the library, beyond the boundaries of what is already known about a subject, in an attempt to discover or create new information. When you do this, you are engaging in "primary" research. Primary research uses firsthand research methods to obtain information from an original source.

The most often used primary research methods for business research purposes are:

a. the sample survey or questionnaire
b. the interview
c. the field experiment
d. the field observation

College and university campuses are often convenient places for the student researcher to learn to employ these methods. The readily available members of the educational community can serve as ideal populations to use for primary research.

For example, if you were setting out to examine the preliminary hypothesis that Americans spend more when purchasing items on credit than they spend when buying with cash, you could attempt to test your hypothesis in these ways:

a. Design and administer a questionnaire intended to reveal purchasing patterns with or without credit.
b. Interview a cross section of the community to learn current attitudes towards the use of credit or cash.
c. Design a simulated experiment intended to test the hypothesis.
d. Obtain permission to observe spending patterns at a point-of-purchase location.

If permission was obtained first, all of these activities could take place within your academic community. However, you should not ignore the research opportunities available in the larger community outside your institution. Business leaders, employees, and customers are all valuable sources of information.

Regardless of which primary research method you use, the success of your efforts will be based on two factors: the reliability and validity of the research process. Reliability is the quality of consistency in the measurement process. Put another way, you or another researcher must be able to repeat the research method and obtain the same results before you can be certain your method is reliable.

Validity is present when your research or measurement method actually measures what you intend to measure. If you set out to measure whether investors are bullish (optimistic) on the direction of the stock market, you must ask questions or use other methods to obtain that information. If, instead, you ask investors which financial news programs they watch on television, your method would lack validity. You would be measuring certain television viewing habits rather than investor attitudes.

Finally, for your primary research to be effective, you must know how to go about using each method. That is the focus of the rest of this chapter.

5.2 UNDERSTANDING SAMPLE SURVEYS

One of the more frequently used primary research techniques is the sample survey. Commonly used by market researchers, surveys are vital to corporate planning and decision making. One of the best known surveys is the Nielsen ratings which examine the television viewing habits of the nation. The results of this survey determine what programs are offered. Student researchers can use the survey method, but first they must understand what makes surveys effective.

The strength of the sample survey is that it allows the researcher insight into the attitudes or preferences of large numbers of people by questioning only a relatively small group. The Nielsen survey is given to just a few thousand families, and yet it claims to be able to pinpoint the TV viewing preferences of an entire country. This is possible due to the *random* way that a sampling of the *population* is selected to be questioned.

To obtain a random sample of any group, you must take steps to see that those questioned are truly representative of the larger group. This is done by ensuring every person an equal chance to participate and by not choosing those to be questioned according to any predetermined pattern of selection. If the selection process for the Nielsen population is indeed random, the participating families should be a true cross-section of Americans and should vary according to age, sex, race, ethnic background, income, education, geographical location, and occupation, as well as other variables.

The researcher next prepares and administers the questionnaire. Here too, there are guidelines to follow if you are to reach your objective. You are after a set of responses that can be collected, tabulated, and analyzed. First, you must design a professional survey.

5.3 PREPARING AND ADMINISTERING SURVEYS

Questionnaires and surveys may be administered by mail, by telephone, or in person. The method you choose will be determined by the nature of your project, along with practical considerations such as logistics, time, and budget constraints. Depending on these variables, there can be advantages or disadvantages to each method. Also, the design of your questionnaire will be slightly different, since the communication environment will vary with each method.

There are, however, some principles of survey question design that have general application. Following these principles will both increase your rate of returns in mail surveys and enhance chances of obtaining reliable replies.

1. List your objectives, the information you wish to obtain. Write questions to accomplish all your objectives.
2. Keep your questions brief. Length discourages those who are under no obligation to answer. If you can do what you need in five questions, don't use ten.
3. Choose clear, precise wording to minimize misunderstanding and misinterpretation. Simplicity of language allows for variations in the educational level of respondents.

4. Arrange your questions in a logical sequence with general questions preceding specific ones.
5. Place attention-getting, high-interest questions first and position the more difficult ones at the end.
6. Be sure your questions are unbiased and do not lead the respondent towards a particular answer or choice. Avoid asking two questions at once.
7. Construct your questions so they may be answered with objective answers (yes-no, multiple choice) or in accordance with a Likert scale for numerical coding.
8. Word your questions so that they do not threaten the respondent. Guarantees of confidentiality also are needed to allay distrust.
9. Be certain your questionnaire is totally professional in its appearance. It must also be free from spelling or grammatical errors.
10. Arrange responses so they may be tabulated easily.

In addition to following these principles, you need to carefully review the population you wish to reach and consider the timing of your survey. Finally, you must provide a cover letter explaining who you are and the purpose of your survey.

5.3.1 Mail Surveys

The mail questionnaire is so commonplace that most adults are familiar with the research method. The reason for this widespread use is that the advantages of the mail survey outweigh the disadvantages. On the plus side, mail surveys allow researcher to contact large numbers of diverse respondents at minimum expense in a short period of time. Confidentiality can more definitely be assured by mail and the respondent can take time to answer. These are obvious advantages compared to telephone or personal interview surveys.

The major disadvantage of the mail survey is that a sufficient number of responses is never guaranteed. Because of this problem, researchers encourage responses by enclosing stamped, preaddressed envelopes to ease return; by simplifying responses; and by offering inducements such as copies of their completed research report if desired. Another weakness is that someone else other than the intended respondent may complete the survey. Further, there is no opportunity to clarify misunderstandings by mail as there is by phone or in person.

The sample questionnaire on page 71 is an example of a survey designed to establish what students know or need to know about managing money. The questions can provide clues to the behavior of students as consumers, and in turn serve as guidelines for course content or programs that might be offered by a student services organization. The questions can be revised as needed.

Figure 10:   Student survey.

	Yes	No	Some-times
1. Do you write down your goals?	___	___	___
2. Do you know how your values and goals influence spending?	___	___	___
3. Do you keep a record of your spending to learn more about your actual spending habits?	___	___	___
4. Do you have a savings fund?	___	___	___
5. Can you list some of the goals you hope to reach within the next year?	___	___	___
6. Do you balance spending with income?	___	___	___
7. Can you adjust your spending plan to meet unexpected situations?	___	___	___
8. Do you keep the items you own in good condition?	___	___	___
9. Do you and your family work together in planning the use of family income?	___	___	___
10. Do you know approximately how much your family spends on you each year?	___	___	___
11. Do you recognize the needs of others in your family?	___	___	___
12. Do you use a shopping list to guide spending and avoid "impulse buying?"	___	___	___
13. Do you know where to find information on goods and services?	___	___	___
14. Do you read labels, tags, and seals attached to products and keep them handy for reference?	___	___	___
15. Do you know when a bargain is a bargain for you?	___	___	___
16. Do you compare prices and quality of different items before you buy?	___	___	___
17. Do you consider wise use of time and energy (human and nonhuman) as well as money when you shop?	___	___	___
18. Is your shopping manner courteous and businesslike?	___	___	___
19. Do you find out the cost of credit before you use it?	___	___	___
20. Do you know what responsibilities you assume in using consumer credit?	___	___	___
21. Do you pay bills promptly?	___	___	___
22. Do you ever read the financial sections in newspapers?	___	___	___
23. Do you know how tax money is used?	___	___	___
24. Do you know how consumer decisions affect business and the economy?	___	___	___
25. Do you know your consumer rights and responsibilities?	___	___	___

Source: Household International: Money Management, page 10, Prospect Heights, IL, 1988.

If such a survey was mailed to a sampling of students, it would be accompanied by a cover letter explaining the purpose of the questionnaire and how the results would be used.

5.3.2 Telephone Surveys

During recent years, the telephone has become a major marketing tool for American businesses. Much of the increased activity has been in direct selling or telemarketing while other activity has focused on marketing research using the telephone survey. Over two million new jobs have been created, and it is anticipated that before the end of the century eight million new positions in the field will be created.

The likely explanation for these increases is that modern business people are no longer willing to wait for information. The telephone allows for instant information, minimizing delays of any kind. This is the advantage of the telephone survey. It can be done now, given the personnel and resources. The problem with the telephone survey is that you run a considerable risk of alienating the interviewer by calling at an inopportune time. Also the absence of face-to-face contact affects the communication. As a result, telephone surveys need to be tightly structured. Ideally, the telephone interviewer will ask a limited number of questions or require simple objective answers.

USA Today conducted a telephone survey to examine the extent to which women have been starting their own businesses. Also, *USA Today* wanted to learn some of the personal characteristics of those women entrepreneurs. A telephone survey consisting of eight questions was conducted, in which 627 National Association of Women Business Owners members were interviewed. The members were chosen at random and contacted over a five-day period. Results of the survey are shown on page 73.

5.3.3 In-Person Surveys

You may find that in-person surveying is the easiest and most economical method to use. Students, staff, and faculty are readily accessible and usually quite willing to cooperate. In addition to these advantages, in-person surveying allows you to clarify any questions the respondent might have.

The disadvantages of the in-person approach should be weighed before you make a choice. For one thing, this method is usually more time- consuming. Another concern is that the lack of confidentiality might alter the responses given, particularly if the subject of the survey is a sensitive one requiring personal answers. A final pitfall is that during the interpersonal exchange, nonverbal communication might generate some bias. This last problem, of course, could not exist during mail or telephone surveys. Despite these possible difficulties, personal contact is an indispensable primary research method.

WOMEN ENTREPRENEURS: WHO ARE THEY?

A business revolution is under way–and women are leading the charge. During the 1980s, women have been starting businesses at twice the rate of men: 4.6 million women own their own firms now vs. 2.5 million in 1980. What type of women are they? Highly educated, extremely self-confident and driven to control their own destinies.

A USA TODAY poll of National Association of Women Business Owners members found these women aren't the mythical spouses who inherit a husband's business. Most–64%–are married, but 53% never spent time as a homemaker. We interviewed 627 NAWBO members at random for the telephone poll from May 22 through 26. The margin of error is plus or minus 4 percentage points.

Why did you start your business?

Answer	Percent responding¹
To prove I could succeed	82%
To control my work schedule	82%
I had a great idea for a business	71%
I encountered promotional barriers	46%
Because I was bored	45%

¹ Respondents could choose more than one

How did you get ownership of your business?

Started it myself 78%
Took over family busines 7%
Bought a franchise 3%
other 4%
Bought it 9%

¹ totals less than 100 due to rounding

How many hours a week do you work?

Answer	Percent responding¹
30 hours or less	4%
31-40 hours	12%
41-50 hours	26%
51-60 hours	33%
61-80 hours	22%
more than 80 hrs	2%

¹ totals less than 100 due to rounding

What was your household income in 1988?

Answer	Percent responding¹
$25,000 or less	3%
$25,001-$50,000	13%
$50,001-$100,00	42%
more than $100,000	42%

What type of business are you in?

Answer	Percent responding¹
Public relations, marketing	20%
data processing	15%
Business Services/Personnel	13%
Finance	11%
Retailing	9%
Medicine/Law	7%
Personal Services, beauty	7%
Visual design	7%
Construction/Real Estate	6%
Manufacturing	5%
Food services	3%
Education/training	1%
Other	5%

¹ totals less than 100 due to rounding

What did you do before owning your own business?

Answer	Percent responding¹
Worked for a large corporation	39%
Worked for a small corporation	28%
Did not work	12%
Worked for the business I now own	33%
Owned another business	9%
Other	3%

¹ totals less than 100 due to rounding

What is your educational level?

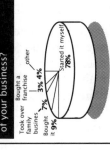

Some high school 2%
High school graduate 3%
Some college 26%
College graduate 37%
Advanced degree 31%

¹ totals less than 100 due to rounding

If you have children younger than age 13, how many hours a week do you work?

Answer	Percent responding¹
30 hours or less	5%
31-40 hours	19%
41-50 hours	30%
51-60 hours	30%
61-80 hours	14%
more than 80 hrs	2%

¹ totals less than 100 due to rounding
Source: USA TODAY poll
By Web Bryant, USA TODAY

Student in-person surveys do not have to be confined to the college campus, as a recent program at a medium-sized northeastern university shows so well. In fact, for this survey it was necessary to go "on the road." As such, this research project can be seen as a combination of an in-person survey with field observation. The results obtained are not so much responses to questions but rather a record of observed experiences.

Johnson & Wales University Most Hospitable Cities Survey

In response to increasing customer service demands and alarming "service gaps" within the hospitality and other service-oriented industries, students from Johnson & Wales University in Providence, Rhode Island, developed the nation's first program for measuring service and hospitality. Known as "America's Most Hospitable Cities Survey," this evaluation program enables students to measure, evaluate, and rate the level of service in major cities around the country. To prepare for the program, students spent an entire semester studying quantitative evaluation techniques, formulating survey criteria, and designing survey questions.

SURVEY DESIGN

Designed by thirteen honor hospitality students, America's Most Hospitable Cities Survey combines students' working knowledge of the restaurant, hotel, recreation, and travel industries. The students identified the criteria for critiquing a city's service. The seminar students completed America's Most Hospitable Cities Survey as their final seminar project.

SURVEY IMPLEMENTATION

The students spend three to four days in each target city identifying key categories that reflect each city's service strengths and weaknesses. To experience each city as thoroughly as possible, students break up into teams. Team members assume the roles of tourists, business travelers, and meeting planners while they measure the service in restaurants, hotels, retail establishments, visitor attractions, and public transportation systems.

On average, students partake in at least 75 percent of the visitor attractions, eat in 75 percent of a city's restaurants, stay in over 90 percent of the hotels, and shop in 75 percent of the retail stores for each target city. In the process, students have thousands of service encounters with hospitality employees in each city they visit.

The survey's rating system uses the same approach as the Mobil Star and AAA diamond ranking. Students award each city a one- to five-pineapple rating, (pineapples are the international hospitality symbol), based on their evaluation showing and numerous service encounters.

Students also choose one individual as the "Most Hospitable Person" in each city they visit. This decision is based on the student's experiences and service encounters.

After the students rate the service of each city they present local government officials and business leaders with tips and strategies for enhancing their city's service.

The student-designed surveys being used in this successful program can be studied as examples of a classroom project which resulted in a program that received considerable national attention.

Figure 11.   America's Most Hospitable Cities Survey Forms

ENCOUNTERS

Your Init.: _____
Date: _____

Place: _____ Situation: _____

Department/Title: _____

Goes above and beyond delivery of service. Positively impacts guest experience.	Delivers personalized service. Attentive and responsive to guest needs.	Delivers services effectively. Responsive to guest needs.	Delivers service inconsistently. Somewhat responsive to guest needs.	Fails to deliver service in a consistent manner. Not responsive to guest needs.	
5	4	3	2	1	N/A

1. COURTESY

___ Reacts to guest in timely manner
___ Acknowledges guests presence in a professional way
___ Appropriately greets guest
___ Interrupts work to politely accommodate guest
___ Demonstrates respect for guest's opinion

2. RESOURCEFULNESS

___ Listens attentively
___ Reads body language
___ Apologizes to guest (if necessary)
___ Empathizes with guest's unique situation
___ Responds appropriately
___ Confidently takes initiative
___ Follows up
___ Knows when to request assistance

3. FRIENDLINESS

___ Projects sincerity/warmth
___ Offers assistance cheerfully
___ Generous with time
___ Enthusiastically approaches task/guest
___ Demonstrates employer loyalty

4. EFFICIENCY

___ Timely performance of function
___ Organized performance of tasks
___ Systematic follow up
___ Demonstrates competency

Outstandingly impacts guest experience	Positively impacts guest experience	Adequately impacts guest experience	Negatively impacts guest experience	Inconsiderate of guest needs	
5	4	3	2	1	N/A

5. PRODUCT KNOWLEDGE   ___ Answers questions accurately
___ Volunteers additional information willingly
___ Suggestive selling
___ Knows unique aspects of facility

6. DEPORTMENT   ___ Poised behavior
___ Appropriate appearance
___ Distinguishable from guests
___ Suitable manner of speech
___ Well groomed/cleancut

7. CONSISTENCY   ___ Remains in control during busy situation
___ Treats guests fairly
___ Performs expected functions
___ Value consistent with cost
___ Adequate service personnel ratio

COMMENTS: _____

_____

_____

SOCIAL ARTIFACTS

Your Unit.: _____
Date: _____

Place: _____ Situation: _____

Outstandingly impacts guest experience	Positively impacts guest experience	Adequately impacts guest experience	Negatively impacts guest experience	Inconsiderate of guest needs	
5	4	3	2	1	N/A

1. COMFORT LEVEL   ___ Noise level
___ Spacing/seating
___ Lighting
___ Temperature controls
___ Cleanliness
___ Ventilation

2. EXTERIOR ACCESSIBILITY   ___ Easy to approach
___ Separate handicapped facilities
___ Visibility/signage
___ Multiple/convenient accesses

3. SAFETY/SECURITY   ___ Adequate lighting
___ Visible signage
___ Active/passive restraints
___ Preventive maintenance
___ Visible security measure
___ Employee awareness of security problems

Outstandingly impacts guest experience	Positively impacts guest experience	Adequately impacts guest experience	Negatively impacts guest experience	Inconsiderate of guest needs	
5	4	3	2	1	N/A

4. PHYSICAL/EXTERIOR ENVIRONMENT
   - ____ Lighting
   - ____ Landscaping
   - ____ Maintenance of physical property
   - ____ Parking availability
   - ____ Suitable location
   - ____ Appropriate amenities and services

5. PHYSICAL INTERIOR ENVIRONMENT
   - ____ Unimpaired traffic flow
   - ____ Maintenance of facility
   - ____ Physical layout
   - ____ Rest room availability
   - ____ Signage
   - ____ Amenities appropriate to facility

COMMENTS: _____

_____

_____

5.4 CONDUCTING PERSONAL INTERVIEWS

Some research projects may be strengthened if you interview an authority in a particular field. If, for instance, your paper is on modern management techniques, why not talk with someone who is known to have expertise in that area? Start by finding out if such a person is on your college or university faculty or in the local business community.

If you are interested in compliance with income tax laws, talk to an Internal Revenue Service agent. If small business is your topic, talk to the owner of a fast-food restaurant. These people are usually willing to share what they have learned or experienced if you conduct the interview professionally. Here are ten suggestions to help you do that.

1. Choose the person to interview based on how he/she can contribute to the achieving of your objectives.
2. Find out as many specific facts about the person as you can. Record the information on a bibliographic card or in your research journal, as you will need it for documentation.
3. Write or telephone the person to request the interview. Estimate the amount of time you will need.
4. Explain the purpose of the interview and any benefit to the interviewee.
5. Assure the interviewee that you will exercise good judgment in using the material from the interview. Perhaps you can offer to let the interviewee approve any quotation before it is used.
6. Prepare a list of questions or subjects to be covered.

7. Listen well and take notes during the interview. If you wish to tape record the interview, ask the interviewee for permission.

8. Stick to your topic. Ask only those questions directly relevant to your purpose.

9. Keep to the time frame that you requested. Be sure that you initiate the end of the interview in a friendly but businesslike manner.

10. Write out your notes in your research journal while they are fresh in your mind immediately after the interview. Send a note to the interviewee thanking him/her for the interview.

5.5 USING OTHER FIELD RESEARCH TECHNIQUES

Psychologists, sociologists, and other social scientists have long used primary research techniques in their work. Generally, this meant engaging in some type of case study (observation) or controlled experiment. Some examples would be sociologists studying particular groups of people (case study) or psychologists testing how a particular variable (e.g., alcohol) would affect behavior (controlled experiment). These same techniques are now widely used by businesses, particularly but not exclusively in marketing and marketing research. They may also be helpful to students conducting business research.

When used for business research, field techniques are generally simpler than social science methods, but the purpose is the same. The business researcher wishes to discover information that will be useful to the overall objective. For instance, supermarket chains send comparison shoppers into competitor stores to determine price levels of products. This "participant" observation represents a rather direct approach to research. Similarly, the highly publicized taste testings between leading soft drink manufacturers are the most basic form of controlled experiment. Both examples *require* that particular field research techniques be used in order to make their point.

As a student preparing to write a business research paper, you need to ask whether the use of a field research technique will help you achieve your project objective. If the answer is yes, then by all means choose a method and use it. Strive for consistency and objectivity in recording your results.

As was stated earlier, campuses are convenient places to conduct sample surveys. The same holds true for observation or experimentation. Attend a men's sporting event and observe the number of women present. Then attend a women's event and count the number of men present. Compare the results to see if there is equal support. Offer two types of candy bars to a representative number of students to determine preference. Count the daily number of students who eat breakfast at the campus dining hall for a week and compare it to the number who have signed up for meal plans. Simple as they may seem, these are all legitimate research methods. Coupled with secondary research, these and other primary methods will help you accomplish your purpose.

5.6 ANALYZING AND EVALUATING PRIMARY INFORMATION

Regardless of the primary research method you use, you must know what to do with your findings. Here are some general guidelines:

1. a. Survey data must be collected, tabulated, and turned into percentages.

   b. Next you need to analyze or interpret the results of your survey to determine significant patterns.

   c. Finally you must decide what impact your findings have on your objective or purpose. Do they confirm your preliminary hypothesis or contradict it?

2. a. Information gathered during interviews must be reviewed carefully, either by rereading your notes or listening to a tape recording.

   b. Decide what statements made by the interviewee are relevant to your purpose and isolate them in your research journal.

   c. Reconfirm that the credentials and experience of your interviewee are such that what you are using from the interview will be considered credible.

3. Observation and experimentation may require combinations of subjective and objective evaluation. In particular, observation may combine some type of tally with a subjective recording of other relevant details. For example, a count of students at athletic events wearing clothes with college or university logos might be accompanied by descriptions of their outward display of school spirit or enthusiasm. Experiments such as taste testings tend to let the results speak for themselves (objective), but certainly some recording of comments during the test might add interest to the project.

In summary, the business researcher needs to be aware of the entire range of primary research methods. Deciding which method to use should be based on many factors, such as the nature of the problem, nature of the data, the nature of the sources, the available resources, and the time constraints. Finally, the business researcher much exercise professional ethics in using any data obtained and avoid the temptation to misuse data to "prove" a hypothesis.

Application Activities

1. List three examples each of primary and secondary research.
2. Label the following sources of information as either primary or secondary.

    a. A personality profile from *Harvard Business Review*.

    b. A taste testing campaign of two soft drinks.

    c. A survey of leisure-time activities of some entrepreneurs.

    d. A biography of a corporate president.

    e. A newspaper report about a business merger.

3. Prepare a five-question minisurvey of students on your campus. Use the ten suggestions in this chapter to help sharpen your survey. Choose from the following survey objectives:

To find out:

    a. What is the highest income they expect to earn in any one year

    b. What average age they expect to retire

    c. The average starting salary they expect to earn immediately after graduation

    d. Whether they expect to attend graduate school

    e. The average number of companies they expect to work for during their careers

4. Interview a member of the business faculty to determine what he/she considers the most promising career opportunities during the next twenty years.

5. Design a field research technique (observation or experiment) to test the preliminary hypothesis that the use of credit increases consumer spending.

6

READING AND TAKING NOTES

Learning Objectives

Upon completing this chapter you should be able to:

1. Use proven reading techniques to make your research most productive.
2. Explain and avoid plagiarism.
3. Compile a working bibliography.
4. Take accurate and complete summary notes, paraphrase notes, direct quotation notes, and combination notes.

6.1 READING SOURCES

You must become an active, selective reader, one who reads a text to find answers to specific research questions. Much like a prospector for gold, you sift through the raw material hoping to locate nuggets of valuable information. You discard that which has no value and set aside that which does for further analysis. Sometimes, you are uncertain of what you have found and you must wait until later in the search for clarification.

Just as the experienced prospector acquired an understanding of the most productive techniques and tools to use, so too must you develop research expertise. You can benefit from the experience of many before you by trying the following proven approaches to reading.

READING TECHNIQUES

1. Get in the practice of *previewing* any article or book before reading the entire text. This means reading the preface or foreword of the book as well as scanning the table of contents and index. It means reading the first and last paragraphs of an article and skimming the text to see

if its content is relevant to your search. Previewing saves time by allowing you to read more selectively.

2. When you find relevant material, photocopy the pertinent sections so that they are yours to work with. Be sure to record the full source information for a later bibliography.

3. As you read, make comments on the margins of your photocopies either posing questions or stating your reactions at the time. Later, when you return to these sources, you will be quickly reminded of their relevance. Highlighting important passages can also be useful as long as you highlight sparingly. Remember, highlighting everything is the same as highlighting nothing.

4. When a book can not be copied or highlighted, use strips of paper to mark specific pages. Later, you may go back to the marked text to extract needed data.

5. Whenever you are researching sources, have your researcher's journal with you as a convenient place to take notes. Avoid the bad habit of jotting down references and notes on the back of notebooks or on random scraps of paper. This most certainly will save later frustration when you begin to organize your paper.

6.2 UNDERSTANDING AND AVOIDING PLAGIARISM

Plagiarism is an act of intellectual dishonesty, in which an individual uses the ideas or statements of another person in such a way as to make it seem as if those ideas or statements are his/her own. Plagiarism may occur unintentionally when a researcher does not understand the need for proper documentation, or intentionally when it is done knowingly. When the latter situation occurs, it is not uncommon for professors to treat plagiarism as a kind of theft and to discipline the plagiarist accordingly.

Since all secondary research consists of reading the works of other writers, student researchers must know how and when to give credit to another author by proper documentation. Here are some basic guidelines to follow:

1. You do not need to document your own ideas or insights or any information which can be considered generally known or "public" information.

2. You do need to document: (a) Ideas of an author that you either summarize or paraphrase. (b) Any quotation you take directly from another author.

Ideally, your final paper will be a blend of your own ideas and those you have discovered during your search. Proper documentation, using one of the systems outlined in chapter 9 of this book, will not only give your work the support of recognized authoritative sources, but it is also the fair and ethical thing to do.

6.3 COMPILING A WORKING BIBLIOGRAPHY

To assemble a working bibliography, go to the appropriate subject headings in the card catalog and look for sources that might be helpful. It is a good idea to identify as many sources as you can from the catalog and begin your long list of sources.

Your instructor may require you to write the bibliographical information on 3 × 5 cards, the traditional system of recording sources. If you have a choice, try to enter each source on a separate page in your researcher's journal. Keeping sources on a separate note page is the more efficient way to keep records for three reasons. First, keeping all your work in the journal reduces the risk of losing information. Another reason is that later on you can add comments and notes about the source under the bibliographic reference if you decide to use that source for your paper. A notebook page allows you more room to do your notetaking. Another advantage is when you have two or more closely related sources, they can be written on the same note page and later used together in the paper.

When you begin your working bibliography, you need not take down all the information that the catalog offers about each source. Initially just write down enough information to help you locate the sources on the shelves in your library: the call number, author(s), and title.

Once you have located the sources on your list and have scanned the tables of contents and indexes, decide which ones will be useful to developing your paper. For those books complete the bibliographical information. Turn to the book's title page and copyright page and take down the following items for each source you expect to use for your paper.

1. author(s) or editor(s)
2. title and subtitle
3. volume number and series
4. place of publisher
5. publisher
6. latest copyright date

From this list you should take down only those items appropriate to your source. When you are ready to assemble your works cited page, all the information for each source will be entered on separate note pages. Details of documentation styles will be discussed in chapter 9.

Call Number	658.001
Bibliographical entries are written out in full here. When Writing works-cited list, use appropriate abbreviations suggested in chapter 9	Miller, Lawrence M. *American Spirit: Visions of a New Corporate Culture.* New York: William Morrow and Company, Inc, 1984. 129–130

a brief note about source   good description—examines
                                   management techniques of
                                   American Corporations

6.4 NOTETAKING SUGGESTIONS

It is a common instructional technique to require undergraduates to use both bibliography cards and summary note cards to record data. Indeed, students often have to turn in these note cards as evidence that their research is progressing well. If you have such a requirement, use either a three-by-five or four-by-six index card; otherwise use your researcher's notebook and follow these suggestions.

1. Before taking a note, write a shortened version of the source to facilitate documentation at a later date, such as: (Peters 144). This will allow you to go to the full bibliography card without delay.
2. Write clear, complete sentences which will be easy to understand when you are actually writing. An abbreviated note may save time now but cause problems later.
3. Try to limit each card to one major point of information.
4. Indicate on the back of the card what part of your paper the note relates to, using your preliminary outline as a guide. You may use the back of the card to record any personal thoughts related to the note.
5. If in doubt about the relevance of certain material, take a note. It is better to have too much information than too little.
6. Be clear as to whether your note is a summary note, a paraphrase note, a direct quotation note, or a combination note.

The following sample notes (summary note, paraphrase note, direct quotation note, and combination note) are based on this passage from *AMERICAN SPIRIT: VISIONS OF A NEW CORPORATE CULTURE* by Lawrence M. Miller. Read the passage looking for key ideas and subordinate ideas that you think would be essential in writing a shortened version of the original. Then compare your notes with those suggested in 6.5, 6.6, 6.7, and 6.8.

THE STRENGTH TO RESPECT

The manager who can be trusted, who possesses integrity, will almost always tend to make positive assumptions about others. The psychological mechanism of projection is at work here. We have a tendency to project feelings about ourselves onto others. If we feel inadequate, disappointed with ourselves, or guilty about some action, we are likely to strike out at others as though they were the cause of these feelings. This mechanism works in positive situations as well. The person who is honest, who is certain of his or her trustworthiness is more likely to see those qualities in others. Rather than assuming that people are devious such a person will assume that they may be trusted. To be able to display respect and appreciation for the positive qualities of others is an indication of one's respect for oneself. Others respond to this behavior intuitively. We intuitively trust the person who has the good judgment to place trust in us. Because we perceive that the other person has high expectations of us, we act to fulfill those expectations. A cycle of trusting and trustworthy behavior is established by the manager who has the strength, the security, and the self-respect that allow him to behave in a trusting way toward others. This is the manager who is able to listen sincerely to the ideas and concerns of others. This is the manager who does not need to take credit for each success but feels most free in passing that credit on to his subordinates. This is the manager who does not require to know every detail of a subordinate's business, because he assumes that the subordinate is capable. This is the manager who does not punish poor performance on the assumption that the individual didn't try hard enough, but problem-solves with that individual to help him on the assumption that the person would perform if he could. This is the manager who displays integrity.

6.5 WRITING A SUMMARY NOTE

A summary restates the original source in your own words as you recall the main points of the text. Thoughtful word choice, sentence structure, and sequencing of ideas are necessary in order to condense the work without altering its meaning. As you summarize, locate key words and main ideas that will give the gist of the information in the article. Do not include details and examples when you summarize.

Remember that failure to document a summary is plagiarism.

Example of Summary Note

Miller, *American* 129–130

According to Miller, managers who possess self-confidence and integrity will have the strength to respect others. They are secure about their capabilities and are trustworthy. How managers feel about themselves has a psychological effect on how they deal with other people. Effective managers who have a positive self-image will perceive positive traits in their subordinates. In turn, the workers will perform tasks in a positive manner and meet the expectations of the manager. When good managers listen to the ideas of the workers and acknowledge good employee performance, the cycle of mutual respect continues between managers and subordinates.

6.6 WRITING A PARAPHRASE NOTE

The paraphrase, like the summary, restates the original source in your own words. A summary identifies the most important ideas in the original, but a paraphrase contains all the information in the original. Usually a paraphrase follows the original writing closely as you translate the author's words line by line. To paraphrase, think about the original meaning of the words, then substitute your own synonyms to express the author's thoughts. If you have difficulty thinking of a synonym on your own, you may consult a dictionary or thesaurus as a last resort. Be sure to choose synonyms that fit the context of the passage. A paraphrase should retain, not distort, the original meaning. Paraphrasing is especially helpful when you are rewriting a lengthy passage. A paraphrase with shorter sentences will simplify the original version.

Remember that failure to document a paraphrase is plagiarism.

Example of Paraphrase Note

Strong managers possess the qualities of self-confidence, self-respect, and self-integrity. They trust their own abilities and are secure in their work. As they take on challenges, they accept their own feelings without becoming discouraged.

Because strong managers are secure with themselves they are capable of passing on those same qualities of respect, trust, and confidence to others. As a result, subordinates feel secure and confident that they are accepted for their positive qualities. The workers are perceived as wanting to function well at their job. In this atmosphere of reciprocal trust, uncritical managers allow workers to do their jobs without scrutiny. The managers trust the workers, and the workers trust the managers.

Strong managers do not criticize poor performance. Instead they work constructively with the person who wishes to perform well. The cycle of trust is reinforced by managers who perceive integrity in others by listening to their suggestions.

6.7 WRITING A DIRECT QUOTATION NOTE

When you quote rather than summarize or paraphrase a source, you wish to retain the vivid language and authoritative expression of the author. If the author has phrased a sentence in a special way, you may choose to quote it rather then rewrite it in your own words. However, factual information should be paraphrased or summarized. When you quote be sure to be accurate. Compare your version carefully with the original for correctness. Use quotation marks to indicate the beginning and ending of the quoted passage, or for longer passages, indent the quoted passages without using quotation marks.

If you choose to omit words in the quotation, use three ellipsis dots (...) to indicate omission. Make sure that what you omit is not essential to the passage or you may risk distorting the complete meaning of the quote. Use quotations sparingly. Do not get into the habit of stringing together quotation after quotation to develop your paper.

Remember that failure to document a direct quotation is plagiarism.

Example of Direct Quotation Note

Miller, *American* 129–130

"The person who is honest, who is certain of his or her trustworthiness is more likely to see those qualities in others."

6.8 WRITING A COMBINATION NOTE

A note may combine summary and quotation. The combination note is very useful because the writer blends his own ideas and expression with a direct quote from the source. Be sure to use quotation marks around key ideas or words of the original source. You should make clear which words are your own and which belong to the source.

Remember that failure to document a combination note is plagiarism.

Example of Combination Paraphrase and Quotation Note

Miller, *American* 129–130

Miller describes a strong manager as one who " . . . is able to listen sincerely to the ideas and concerns of others."

Application Activities

1. On a single page in your researcher's journal, write a bibliographical entry for the following:

   The source is a book by Peter F. Drucker entitled *The Frontiers of Management: Where Tomorrow's Decisions Are Being Shaped Today*. The place of publication is New York by Truman Talley Books/ E.P. Dutton, with a 1986 copyright. Your reference is to information taken from pages 182–183. The book's call number is HD31 .D7713.

2. In your researcher's journal prepare four different notes from the passage by Peter F. Drucker. Use a separate page for each of the following:

   a. Write a summary note.
   b. Write a paraphrase note.
   c. Write a direct quotation note.
   d. Write a combination note.

Drucker, *Frontiers* 182–183

In Japanese law, as in American and European law, management is the servant of the stockholders. But this the Japanese treat as pure fiction. The reality which is seen as guiding the behavior of Japanese big-business management (even in companies that are family-owned and family-managed like Toyota) is management as an organ of the business itself. Management is the servant of the going concern, which brings together in a common interest a number of constituencies: employees first, then customers, then creditors, and finally suppliers. Stockholders are only a special group of creditors, rather than "the owners" for whose sake the enterprise exists. As their performance shows, Japanese businesses are not run as philanthropies and know how to obtain economic results. In fact, the Japanese banks, which are the real powers in the Japanese economy, watch economic performance closely and move in on a poorly performing or lackluster top management much faster than do the boards of Western publicly held companies. But the Japanese have institutionalized the going concern and its values through lifetime employment, under which the employees' claim to job and income comes first—unless the survival of the enterprise itself is endangered.

The Japanese formulation presents very real problems, especially at the time of rapid structural change in technology and economy when labor mobility is badly needed. Still, the Japanese example indicates why management legitimacy is a problem in the West. Business management in the West (and in particular business management in the United States) has not yet faced up to the fact that our society has become a society of organizations, of which management is the critical organ.

3. Photocopy and submit a paragraph from a book or article that you have considered using for your research paper. Write a summary note, a paraphrase note, a direct quotation note, and a combination note for that same paragraph.

7
WRITING
EFFECTIVELY

Learning Objectives

Upon completing this chapter you should be able to:

1. Use language that will communicate your message clearly.
2. Blend sentence types for variety and rhythm.
3. Write unified and coherent paragraphs.
4. Organize your research papers by paragraph type.
5. Write in a non-sexist style.

Once your research is completed and information collected in notes that are easily accessible, you are ready to begin writing. As you will see in chapter 8, you will write your business research paper in three distinct stages: prewriting, writing, and revising. All three are necessary to your objective, which is to write a high-quality paper. To further ensure that success, it is helpful to first review the fundamental principles of effective writing. Remember that even though your research is thorough, you have a further obligation to communicate your findings and conclusions in a clear and pleasing style. The logical place to begin this review is with the most basic component of all writing, language.

7.1 WORDS

Did you know that the English language contains over one million words, more than any other language on earth? This gives the writer a seemingly endless assortment of words from which to choose. Does it follow then that effective writing means dazzling the reader with the widest variety of language choices available? Before you answer that question, consider this next statistic. The average adult has a vocabulary of between twenty thousand to thirty thousand words. Now the answer should be more apparent. Consider your audience and use language that will best communicate your message in a clear and unambiguous way. In practice, this means writing in a simple, straightforward style which is direct and easy to read. Here are some suggestions to help you do this.

7.1.1 Using Natural Vocabulary to Enhance Clarity

A key rule about word choice is to avoid the artificial, lengthier words that readers may be uncomfortable with and instead choose the simpler, shorter words that are more familiar. For some reason, many students and business people believe that using longer, more sophisticated words is necessary to impress others. They pore through dictionaries to find longer synonyms for perfectly suitable words. This is a mistake. Synonyms are very useful to the writer. They help the writer avoid repeating words and phrases that might otherwise become tiresome to the reader. Sometimes, synonyms allow the writer to choose the word that has the exact meaning intended. However a synonym should never be used just because it is longer than another word.

Language usage, as with everything else in our culture, has changed rapidly in recent years. One of the major changes has been a movement away from using unnecessarily formal words when writing. Instead, the new emphasis is on informal, natural language that is suitable to your purpose. This suggestion should not be misunderstood. Writing is still a more formal level of communication than conversation, but it is not as formal as it once was. The change is for the better. Gone are the long-winded phrases of the past. A modern writing style is clear and to the point.

The secret to formal or informal language choice is to adapt your style to the type of writing you are doing, in much the same way as you choose different wardrobes for different social occasions. When you have your first on-campus job interview, you won't wear the same outfit that you wear each day to class, will you? It is the same way with words. A business research paper may require some more formal language choices than a business memorandum, but the new emphasis is on a more natural style as long as that style does not lapse into conversational writing or slang.

Self Check

Rewrite each of the sentences below, substituting more natural vocabulary choices for obscure or more formal ones. Use a dictionary or thesaurus, if necessary.

1. The financier had a reputation for being munificent.

_____

_____

2. Her stockbroker was a neophyte in the business.

_____

_____

3. Price-fixing is often done during clandestine meetings of two or more competitors.

_____

_____

4. The transactions between broker and client should be held in the strictest of confidence.

_____

_____

5. Credit card customers need to be advised of any forthcoming clearance of merchandise.

_____

_____

7.1.2 Avoiding Wordiness

You already know that a modern writing style is economical. Stated another way, this means saying what needs to be said in as few words as possible. Unfortunately, this is easier said than done. Since wordiness is one of the most common problems in writing, its causes and solutions need to be examined.

The principal cause of wordiness is a lack of preparation. (This preparation, called prewriting, is discussed in chapter 8.) The writer who does not prepare to write is like the student who, when called upon in class to answer a question, begins to respond without gathering his/her thoughts. Too often, the student's reply wanders in many directions without ever reaching the point. What that student should do is to take a moment to formulate an answer before responding. So, too, should the writer take time to plan what is to be said. Otherwise, the result is likely to be conversational, wordy prose.

To overcome wordiness, the writer must not only engage in careful prewriting but must also do the following:

1. Eliminate unnecessary words, reduce clauses and phrases to words, and omit unimportant, unnecessary facts or details.
2. Avoid redundancy. Do not use two or more words to do the job of one: anticipate in advance, cooperate together, and necessary essentials are examples of redundancies.

3. Use active verbs in place of passive. The dresses were sent by the manufacturer from the plant last Friday (passive verb—twelve words). The manufacturer sent the dresses last Friday (active verb—seven words).

In his essay, "Rewriting," William Zinsser warns against wordiness:

Clutter is the disease of American writing. We are a society strangling in unnecessary words, circular constructions, pompous frills and meaningless jargon....But the secret of good writing is to strip every sentence to its cleanest component. Every word that serves no function, every long word that could be a short word, every adverb which carries the same meaning that is already in the verb, every passive construction that leaves the reader unsure of who is doing what—these are the thousand and one adulterants that weaken the strength of a sentence....(Zinsser 7)

Zinsser's words are right on target. Remember that brevity is the best way to achieve clarity.

Self Check

Rewrite each of the sentences below, editing it so that its main point comes through simply and clearly. Select your words carefully, cutting down their number without altering meaning.

1. In the professional world of lawyers, doctors, and engineers, there are fewer women than men in these areas of concentration.

   _____

   _____

2. Interpersonal communication skills are the necessary essentials of business success.

   _____

   _____

3. Accounting firms need to establish reputations for having the highest integrity if they are to be considered trustworthy.

   _____

   _____

4. New employees should contact the Human Resources Department if they desire additional information on the subject of fringe benefits or any other aspect of employment.

   _____

   _____

5. The negotiations were postponed until after the start of the New Year which is just a month away.

_____

_____

7.1.3 Avoiding Jargon and Cliches

Jargon is the misuse of technical language or terms that pertain exclusively to some special field of interest. Jargon is sometimes acceptable if your audience is composed of people in the same work or people with the same interests. If, however, your audience is not knowledgeable about your subject, meaning is lost when you use jargon.

The words "bull," "call," "put," "bear," and "odd lot" are examples of the jargon of the stock market. If your business research topic is some aspect of the stock market, you must ask yourself whether your audience will be familiar with the special vocabulary you wish to employ. If your audience is unfamiliar with such terms, try to avoid using them. If you must use jargon, provide an accompanying explanatory definition to help understanding. For example: "A person who is an optimist about the future direction of the stock market is called a "bull," one who believes stock prices will rise."

Similarly, eliminate cliches from your writing. Cliches are words or phrases that have been used too often and have lost their original freshness and appeal. The uninspired mind turns to them as a substitute for original thinking. While cliches are occasionally acceptable in casual conversation, there should be no place for them in your writing. Put on paper, cliches have a deadening effect on your writing, making it seem stale and flat. Exclude them from your writing vocabulary and find fresh alternative expressions. Instead of: "That corporation is growing by leaps and bounds", try "That corporation's growth rate is quite rapid."

Self Check

Revise the following sentences, changing or providing clarifying explanations for any jargon you find. Also, substitute fresh, imaginative expressions or simple, direct terms for any cliches.

1. Collecting money from that company is like pulling teeth.

_____

_____

2. That bank is now charging two points for its residential mortgages.

_____

_____

3. No-load mutual funds are thought to be excellent investments.

_____

_____

4. The long arm of the law caught up with the brokers involved with inside trading.

_____

_____

5. To make a long story short we intend to narrow our product line.

_____

_____

7.1.4 Use Specific, Concrete Language

If, as a writer, you wish to keep readers interested, you have a much better chance of doing so if you consciously choose tangible, exact words in place of more abstract general ones. This is much repeated advice given by teachers of writing to their students and for good reason. Words that hook the reader's mind and senses result in a more involved reader. Conversely, vague, non-specific language often has the opposite effect. Lacking something particular to identify with, the reader's attention may wander.

Keep your reader interested by using specific nouns and adjectives as well as supplying precise details that bring a sentence to life.

Example: (Vague) Recently, he worked in the city for a department store.

(Specific) Bill Robinson worked as a coat buyer of ready-to-wear for Macy's in New York City from 1989 to 1990.

Self Check

Rewrite the following sentences to make them more specific and precise. Change whatever words you have to and invent any specific details you need.

1. One large retailer announced a cutback of employees at two locations.

_____

_____

2. All members of the sales force will be given company cars.

_____

_____

3. Certain personality traits are helpful to students who hope to be managers.

_____

_____

4. The oil company's trucks are colorful.

_____

_____

5. That company has an informal dress code for both men and women.

_____

_____

7.2 SENTENCES

The next logical step to effective writing is to master the sentence. As you know, sentences contain two major parts, the subject and the predicate. The subject is the part of the sentence about which you are writing. The predicate is the verb and related words that put action into the sentence or make a statement about the subject.

Subject   Predicate

The woman in the black dress/is an accountant.

Accounting/is a prestigious profession.

As you work to improve your sentence skills, remind yourself of Mark Twain's advice: "The way to write is to write short, simple sentences...." That advice makes sense. Think of any skill you currently have. How did you acquire and develop it? If you are like most people, you probably learned the basics first and then advanced to more complex skills. That is the way to learn to write well. Demonstrate that you can write clear brief sentences first; then, and only then, are you ready to progress to the longer, more involved sentence structures.

7.2.1 Use Subject-Verb Construction

The best way to write clear, brief sentences is to put the subject at the front of your sentence and position the verb shortly after the subject. This is the most natural way to construct a sentence. It is the pattern most people use when they speak, and it will help you avoid lengthier, more involved constructions that you might not yet be able to control. Notice how subject-verb construction is more effective in the following sentences:

Subject-Verb: The corporation postponed its annual meeting until the president returned from a conference in Europe.

Other: Because the president was participating in a European conference, the corporation postponed its annual meeting until he could be in attendance.

Subject-Verb: Mary Collins sells life insurance.

Other: Since Mary Collins sells life insurance, she is continually looking for prospects.

Reread the above examples. See that the subject-verb constructions are clearer and less wordy. Obviously, not every sentence you write will follow this pattern, but most of your sentences should. It is the best way.

Self Check

Rewrite the following sentences using the suggested subject-verb construction. Make any other changes that will improve the sentences.

1. After this quarter's earnings report, the stock of our company should rise.

2. Being that the church is a nonprofit organization, it is exempt from paying taxes.

3. Much earlier in this century, the assembly line was introduced by Henry Ford to mass produce automobiles.

4. Because there was a tear in the pocket, the woman returned the coat to the store.

5. More and more these days students are earning graduate degrees in business-related majors.

7.2.2 Four Types of Sentences

Whenever you begin to write, you should make a choice of what types of sentences to write. There are only four types of sentences in the English language. An essential step toward becoming a skilled writer is learning how to write all four types. Once that is accomplished, you will then be able to vary sentence types for interest and rhythm.

The essential difference among the four sentence types is their number and kind of clauses. A clause is a group of words that contains a subject and a predicate. An independent clause is a complete thought and can stand alone as a simple sentence. A dependent or subordinate clause is not a complete thought. If left by itself, the dependent clause will be a sentence fragment.

- The stock market crashed in October of 1987. (Independent clause as simple sentence)
- After the stock market crashed in October of 1987. (Dependent clause as sentence fragment)

7.2.3 The Simple Sentence

The simple sentence is the basic sentence pattern of one independent clause. Its essence is the subject and verb, but it also may contain modifiers, complements, and other related words. All of the following are simple sentences.

1. He sells.
2. He is a salesman.
3. He sells farm equipment.

7.2.4 The Compound Sentence

The compound sentence consists of two or more independent clauses that are joined by coordinating conjunctions (the most frequently used are "and," "but," and "or") or punctuation marks (colon or semicolon). Generally, the complete thoughts being linked are of comparable importance. All of the following are compound sentences.

1. He sells tractors, but he once worked in a factory.
2. Tractor sales have been increasing, and the trend is likely to continue.
3. Successful selling requires motivation; motivation stems from the desire to be successful.

7.2.5 The Complex Sentence

The complex sentence contains one independent clause and one or more dependent clauses that are joined by subordinating conjunctions or relative pronouns. The dependent clause usually expresses a thought of lesser importance than the independent clause. The complex sentence is more involved than the previous two sentence types and requires greater care if it is to be used properly. Note the different positions of the dependent clauses in the following complex sentences.

dependent clause
1. *If you finish college,* your lifetime earnings are likely to be considerably higher than the non-graduate.

dependent clause
2. The graduate *who possesses strong communication skills* will do well in interviews.

dependent clause
3. Career placement offices list the companies *who will be interviewing on campus.*

7.2.6 The Compound-Complex Sentence

The compound-complex sentence contains two or more independent clauses and one or more dependent clauses. As its name suggests, it is a combination of the previous two sentence types.

The compound-complex sentence is the most involved of all the sentence types and requires the most skill to use effectively. It is also the most difficult to write properly and the most likely to decrease clarity. Consequently, this sentence type should be used less frequently than the others. The following sentences are all compound-complex.

1. Corporate interviewers want to hire qualified applicants who will perform their jobs well, and to do this, interviewers employ different techniques.
2. Some companies require multiple interviews, and the actual hiring decision is made by a group or committee that consists of all those who have conducted the interviews.
3. Others engage in "stress" interviews, while some companies ask the job candidate to participate in social occasions, and through these processes, the interviewer hopes to learn enough to make a decision.

Self Check

Identify each of the following sentences according to sentence types. Use the symbols: (S) simple, (CP) compound, (CX) complex, and (CP-CX) compound-complex.

1. Business cycles are normal, and they should be expected.

_____

_____

2. When recessions occur, the stock market's performance is usually sluggish.

_____

_____

3. Blue-chip stocks should be held for the long term.

_____

_____

4. Mutual funds are sound investments for the individual because they provide professional management, and they also offer diversified investments.

_____

_____

7.2.7 Blending Sentence Types for Variety and Rhythm

The reason you need to be able to recognize and manage all four sentence types is not just an academic one. Indeed, the reason is quite practical. You are now able to make _conscious decisions_ about the sentences you use. Once you reach this point, you have gained _control_ of your writing. You can mold your writing to suit your purpose.

If your sole objective was to write clearly, you could use only short simple and compound sentences which every reader would understand. Unfortunately, this is too simplistic a solution. Such a grouping of sentences might be clear, but they would be boring. They create a repetitive, staccato rhythm which sounds like a drum being beaten over and over again. The way to avoid this staccato effect is to deliberately vary the type of sentence structures you use. Yes, you should use the simple and compound sentences more frequently, as they tend to be clearest, but you must change your rhythm by using complex and compound-complex sentences as well. The key principle to remember is not to use any one sentence type repetitively. Be certain to change sentence length and never write a series of lengthy complex or compound-complex sentences.

Self Check

Each writer has his/her own writing style. Part of this distinctive style is the rhythmic pattern caused by the sentence types chosen. If you wish to see your own rhythmic pattern, take any paragraph that you have written recently or, if you don't have one, write an eight to twelve sentence paragraph on any topic (i.e., career objectives). Use the symbols S, CP, CX, and CP-CX to chart your own "rhythm print." If the chart indicates that you have used the same sentence type repetitively, you may need to concentrate on varying sentence types.

7.3 THE NEED FOR PARAGRAPHS

Paragraphs are as necessary to high-quality writing as are effective word choices and solid sentences. Your research paper is a collection of major ideas, and generally, each major idea requires a separate paragraph. That is one major reason for paragraphs: the need to subdivide your writing into separate concepts. Another equally important justification is that paragraphs aid understanding. Tests prove that comprehension suffers from the absence of paragraphs, and readers react unfavorably to larger blocks of writing that are not broken down into smaller sections.

7.3.1 Paragraph Parts

Paragraphs come in a variety of lengths. Average length paragraphs in research papers range from six to twelve sentences, but these guidelines are flexible. What is less flexible, however, is that all but the briefest paragraphs contain three types of sentences: the topic sentence which states the major idea, supporting sentences which offer facts and examples to explain the topic sentence, and concluding or transitional sentences which finish your thought or provide a link to the next paragraph.

Self Check

Underline the topic sentence in these jumbled paragraphs; sentences are not in their original order. Circle supporting sentences.

1. Part-time jobs are also valuable, especially those requiring interpersonal communication skills. Community and volunteer work can also help. There are still many ways to gain insight into possible careers. Finally, it makes sense to talk to people who are already doing the work you are considering. One of the best ways is to obtain a summer internship.

2. Nothing is certain in life, but taking a logical approach to such a major decision makes more sense than accepting a job based on chance or social pressure. Think about this statistic: only one in every five Americans is happy with his/her job. Since work is such an important part of our lives, more needs to be done to match individual talents with the right positions. Career planning should begin in your freshman year. Ideally, this will result in your career contributing to a happy and purposeful life.

7.3.2 Unity and Coherence in the Paragraph

The easiest way to determine whether your paragraphs are unified is to check whether all other sentences in the paragraph relate directly or indirectly to the topic sentence. Earlier, you learned that the topic sentence states the paragraph's major idea. Any sentence not relevant to the topic sentence violates paragraph unity, and the attentive reader will realize something is wrong. Resist the temptation to stray too far from the subject at hand. In other words, STICK TO THE TOPIC.

Coherence in paragraphs means that the sentences are sequenced so that your ideas flow smoothly and logically. Relationships between ideas are made clear by links that connect sentences into a harmonious whole. Coherence is necessary for clarity and can be achieved by using four basic techniques:

1. Linking major ideas by repetition.
2. Being consistent with use of verb tenses and pronouns.
3. Arranging ideas in logical sequence.
4. Using transitional words or phrases.

Self Check

Rewrite the following paragraph, eliminating any sentence that damages unity. Rearrange the sentences or make other changes to improve coherence.

Employment interviews can cause nervousness and anxiety which, if not controlled, can interfere with your performance during the interview. Knowing this, you need to try to reduce the effects of stress. When you are job hunting, get a good night's sleep and exercise regularly. Feeling healthy and knowing that you look your best can help your confidence. Dress appropriately. Be on time, and when you meet the interviewer, smile and firmly shake his or her hand. For men the most appropriate dress is a navy blue suit, white shirt, striped tie, and black dress shoes. Relax and enjoy the experience. Women have more flexibility, but a conservative dress or suit is best. Show your enthusiasm; use positive language. You can always change career paths later on, and in fact, most people do so more than once.

7.4 ORGANIZING YOUR RESEARCH PAPER BY PARAGRAPH TYPE

Before your conclude your review of paragraphs, it is helpful to see the different types of paragraphs that you will need to write in your business research paper. As you will see in the next chapter, you will require an organizational plan. Remember that all good writing contains a beginning, a middle, and an end. This three-part construction is essential to the success of your paper. Because each of the parts will differ from one another in purpose, each will require different kinds of paragraphs.

7.4.1 Introductory Paragraphs

The beginning or introductory section of a research paper will usually consist of a few paragraphs. One purpose of this section is to get the reader's attention and interest. The method that you use to attract attention and interest will vary with your purpose, but frequently used techniques include citing dramatic facts or posing stimulating questions.

Regardless of the technique used to get attention and interest, your introductory paragraphs should also contain a thesis statement that states the central or controlling idea of the research paper. This is what you are about to develop in the middle paragraphs.

7.4.2 Middle Paragraphs

The middle section or body of your research paper is the largest part of your three-part construction. It is the part that provides supporting evidence for your three-part construction. To develop this section, you will need to use facts, examples, relevant anecdotes, or other explanatory material. Keep these suggestions in mind as you write middle paragraphs:

1. Quantity and quality are essential to the presentation of factual evidence. You must give the reader enough reasons from reputable, verifiable sources if you wish to be effective.
2. Use very specific examples. Avoid vague abstractions.
3. Use only anecdotes or illustrations relevant to your thesis sentences. This preserves unity.
4. Position your paragraphs in logical sequence, saving your most important points for last.
5. Use transitional devices to connect paragraphs. Repeat a word used in the previous paragraph, carry down an idea from one paragraph to the next, or use transitional words (*however, so, despite, therefore, even though,* and *consequently* are some commonly used transitions).

7.4.3 Concluding Paragraphs

Your research paper will require considerable time and effort. Having expended that time and effort, you want your finished work to have impact. To do this, work hard at perfecting the end of your essay so that the reader has something significant to take away.

Concluding paragraphs need to be forceful and to the point in order to have impact. Be succinct, remembering that final impressions stay with readers the longest. Depending on the subject of your research paper, one of these approaches should be suited to your concluding paragraphs:

a. Offer solutions to a problem the paper has identified.
b. Restate your thesis in a slightly different way.
c. End with a question, a strategy which keeps the reader's mind working on your ideas.
d. Summarize major points that were made in the paper.

Self Check

Identify each of the following paragraphs as introductory (I), middle (M), or concluding (C), based on your understanding of each type of paragraph. Look for word or contex clues for each identification. Paragraphs are excerpts from a student research paper.

Those who actually plan to go into business may choose catering, since it requires a small initial investment. Often, this is due to the fact that a very limited inventory is required and the premise may be rented, not necessarily owned. Catering also requires less heavy equipment such as steam tables, large walk-in refrigerators, freezers, and dining room set-up. Since the equipment needed is less, the cost of opening is reduced.

A contract should be part of the planning that goes into the catering of an affair. The contract states how many guests will be present, the type of service that is required, the date, the time, and any additional services that may be provided to the guest by the caterer.

The contract helps take the guesswork out of catering, thereby making it easier to plan than other businesses. Furthermore, it is easier to staff and purchase food, since you will know in advance exactly how much of each is required. This often reduces and may eliminate waste which will decrease profits. One word of caution however: the caterer should remember that he/she is also bound by a contract. The contract should be honored at all times since this is a legal obligation.

Overall, you can see that catering requires very little formal education. It does, however, require interpersonal skills and a culinary background. Catering offers the following advantages: self employment, a smaller initial investment, and less heavy equipment. Establishing your catering set-up will depend on the type of clientele and your target market. These factors are why catering is one of the easiest and the least expensive of all of the food service industries to begin.

Have you ever thought about going into business for yourself? If you have, perhaps catering is the business for you. Catering is one of the easiest and least expensive of all food service industries. It requires fewer skills and a smaller initial investment than other food service businesses. The choice of location is primarily up to you, and since there is usually a predetermined clientele the risk is minimal. Often, the guesswork is taken out of catering by using contracts between the customer and the establishment. What do you think now?

7.5 USE NONSEXIST LANGUAGE

The suggestions made so far are the keys to an effective writing style. As such, they have been part of writing scholarship for a long time. What follows, the call for a nonsexist writing style, is more recent. The reasons for such a call are more socio-cultural than literary. Language usually reflects the dominant values during any particular time period. As such, it is logical to expect that whenever widespread, significant changes take place in a society, changes in language will follow. This has been the case in our society.

The 1960s brought a shift from our previously male-dominated society to a more egalitarian one in which women were recognized as equals. It was a time in which individual rights for members of minority groups were championed. Sensitivity to discrimination in all areas of life was heightened. This included language, and gradually, sexist language gave way to a modern nondiscriminatory style which is more gender-neutral.

Perhaps the easiest way to acquire a nonsexist style is to begin by recognizing its predecessor, a sexist style. In the past, our language mirrored male dominance. From the dropping of the female's family name at marriage to the use of "girl" to describe an adult woman, examples appear everywhere. Writers regularly used masculine singular pronouns and the word "man" generically as well as other constructions that implied that men did all the things of any consequence. Sexual stereotyping was commonplace, suggesting that certain roles were exclusively male (i.e., the professions, law, accounting, medicine, etc.) and others female (i.e., homemaking, child rearing, secretarial work, etc.). In short, language supported the inequality present in the larger society. Today, all of that has changed, and if you wish to be modern, you must adopt the suggestions that follow.

Summary of Guidelines for Nonsexist Language

AMERICAN PHILOSOPHICAL ASSOCIATION – Virginia Warren, Author

When constructing examples and theories, remember to include those human activities, interests, and points of view that traditionally have been associated with females.
Eliminate the generic use of *he* by:

- using plural nouns
deleting *he, his,* and *him* altogether
- substituting articles (*the, a, an*) for *his*; and *who* for *he*
- substituting *one, we,* or *you*
- minimizing use of indefinite pronouns (e.g., *everybody, someone*)
using the passive voice (use sparingly)
- substituting nouns for pronouns (use sparingly)

Eliminate the generic use of *man*:

- for *man*, substitute *person/people, individual(s), human(s), human being(s)*
- for *mankind*, substitute *humankind, humanity, the human race*
- for *manhood*, substitute *adulthood, maturity*
- delete unnecessary references to generic *man*

Eliminate sexism when addressing persons formally by:

- using *Ms* instead of *Miss* or *Mrs*, even when a woman's marital status is known
- using a married woman's first name instead of her husband's (e.g., *Ms. Annabell Lee*, not *Mrs. Herman Lee*)
- using the corresponding title for females (*Ms., Dr., Prof.*) whenever a title is appropriate for males
- using *Dear Colleague* or *Editor* or *Professor*, etc. in letters to unknown persons (instead of *Dear Sir, Gentlemen*)

Eliminate sexual stereotyping of roles by:

- using the same term (which avoids the generic *man*) for both females and males (e.g., *department chair* or *chairperson*), or by using the corresponding verb (e.g., *to chair*)
- not calling attention to irrelevancies (e.g., *lady lawyer, male nurse*)

Direct quotations may not be altered; where appropriate, paraphrase using nonsexist language.

Examples of Sexist Language with Nonsexist Alternatives

EXAMPLE	PREFERRED ALTERNATIVE	COMMENT
GENERIC *HE*		
1. The philosopher uses his reason to guide him.	Philosophers use their reason to guide them.	Use plural nouns.
	OR: The philosopher uses reason as a guide.	Delete *he, his,* or *him* altogether, rewording if necessary.
2. The student did it and he was glad.	The student did it and was glad.	Delete *he*, using compound verbs.
3. The department chair must submit his bjudget by March 1st.	The department chair must submit a budget by March 1st.	Use articles (*the, a, an*) instead of personal pronouns.
	OR: The budget must be submitted by the department chair by March 1st.	Use passive voice for verbs. (Use sparingly.)
4. If the writer plans ahead, he will save a lot of effort.	The writer who plans ahead will save a lot of effort.	Use *who* for *he*.
5. Take seriously what your dean says about falling enrollments. He knows about current demographic trends.	Take seriously what your dean says about falling enrollments. This person knows about current demographic trends.	Substitute a noun for the pronoun. (Use sparingly.)

6. and 7. Minimize the use of indefinite pronouns (*everyone, everybody, someone/body, anyone/body, no one, nobody, another*), all of which take 'he' as a referent.

EXAMPLE	PREFERRED ALTERNATIVE	COMMENT
6. As someone grows older, he grows more reflective.	As one grows older, one grows more reflective.	Use *one, you, we* instead of indefinite pronouns.
	OR: In growing older, people grow more reflective.	Or reword, deleting pronouns altogether.
	CONTROVERSIAL (FOR INFORMAL CONTEXTS ONLY): As someone grows older, they grow more reflective.	The National Council of Teachers of English (1975, p. 3) says, "In all but strictly formal usage, plural pronouns have become acceptable substitutes for the masculine singular" following an indefinite pronoun. Kett and Underwood (1978, p. 38) predict that such informal usage will eventually become acceptable in all contexts.
7. Students are different: one may be assertive in his interpersonal relations, while another may be timid in his approach to the world.	Students are different: one may relate to others assertively, while another may approach the world timidly.	Delete *his*, rewording.
	OR: Students are different: one may be assertive in his or her interpersonal relations, while another may be timid in approaching the world.	Use *he or she, his or her* sparingly, in conjunction with other methods. (*Himself or herself* is awkward. *S/he* breaks down when one comes to *her/his*.) *She or he* and *her or him* are fine. Be consistent: do not begin by useing *he or she* and lapse into the generic *he*. Avoid *he (she), men (and women)*, etc., since including females parenthetically suggests that females are an afterthought.
	OR: Students are different: one may be assertive in her interpersonal relations, while another may be timid in his approach to the world.	Alternate masculine and feminine pronouns when giving examples. (CAUTION: Avoid reinforcing sexual stereotypes. Switching *her* and *his* in ther preferred alternative results in a sentence as sexist as the original.)

8. Use the above methods to avoid the generic *she* for traditionally female occupations. "When a nurse comes on duty she..." is as sexist as "When a physician comes on duty he..."

EXAMPLE	PREFERRED ALTERNATIVE	COMMENT
GENERIC *MAN*		
9. Consider what the ordinary (common) man thinks about justice.	Consider what ordinary people (individuals) think about justice.	Using the plural noun avoids the generic *he* later on.
10. Reason is what distinguishes man from other animals.	Reason is what distinguishes humans (human beings) from other animals.	When *man* is used to contrast species, substitute *humans* or *human beings*.
11. For Aristotle, man is, above all, Political Man.	Aristotle regarded human beings as inherently political.	No nonsexist counterparts to *PoliMan, Economic Man,* etc. preserve the exact flavor of these terms, perhaps because they focus on stereotypically male behavior. Note that much of *Economic Woman's* labor is still unpaid, and hence is excluded from the GNP. Sexist language may camouflage a theory's sexist assumptions.
12. the brotherhood of man feelings of brotherhood or fraternity the Founding Fathers the Father of relativity theory	the human family feelings of kinship, solidarity, affection, collegiality, unity, congeniality, community the Founders (founding leaders) the founder (initiator) of relativity theory	
ADDRESSING THE PROFESSIONAL 13. SALUTATIONS IN BUSINESS LETTERS		
Dear Sir, gentlemen (to an unknown person) Dear Sir, Dear Mr. Green (when first name and sex are unknown)	Dear Colleague, Dear Editor, Dear Professor, Dear Staff Member, etc. Dear Professor (Doctor, Editor) Green, Dear J. Green	Do not presume that people are male until proven otherwise. Do not use *Dear Sir* or *Gentlemen* just because you are sure that there are no women on that committee. If *To Whom It May Concern* seems too brusque and all else fails, adopt a modified memo style (*Attention: Order Department*) or omit the salutation entirely.
Dear Mrs. Green (when a female's marital status is unknown)	Dear Ms. Green, Dear J. Green, Dear Jean Green	Do not presume that women are married until proven otherwise.

EXAMPLE	PREFERRED ALTERNATIVE	COMMENT
14. man and wife men...ladies; or men... girls three male students and two coeds	husband and wife men...women five students (two females and three males)	Of course, if the ages are right, *men...girls* may be appropriate, as may *women ...boys.*
15. males and females husbands and wives men and women sons and daughters descendants of Adam and Eve his and her	females and males wives and husbands women and men daughters and sons descendants of Eve and Adam her and his	Varying the order (if the content does not requre the conventional order) both counters the implication that males take priority over females and enlivens discourse by avoiding cliché.
16. Congressman, Congresswoman	U.S. Representative, mem- ber of Congress	Choose nonsexist labels for occupations.
poetess, stewardess, fireman, lady lawyer, male nurse, woman doctor	poet, flight attendant, fire- fighter, lawyer, nurse, doctor	The terms *lawyer, nurse,* and *doctor* include both males and females.
17. CHOICE OF ADJECTIVES		
cautious men and timid women ambitious men and ag- gressive women [Example 17 is from American Psychologi- cal Association (1977).]	cautious women and men; cautious people; timid men and women; timid people ambitious men and women; ambitious people; aggres- sive women and men; ag- gressive people	Choose adjectives carefully. Sometimes we intend to at- tribute the same trait to fe- males and males; yet, through choosing two ster- eotyped adjectives, we im- ply either that the two groups have different traits or that readers should eval- uate the same trait differ- ently for females and for males. (Note: some adjec- tives have a different emo- tive or descriptive meaning when predicated of one sex or the other.)

Self Check

Rewrite each sentence avoiding sexist language.

1. A lady lawyer must spend much of her time researching a case.

_____

_____

2. Any student registering late for class should see his academic advisor.

_____

_____

3. Each individual should be responsible for making his own career choice.

_____

4. The mailman was unaware of the approaching German shepherd.

_____

5. The chairman of the department prepared his agenda for the meeting.

_____

6. The child is influenced by his parents.

_____

7. He is a male nurse.

_____

8. The Little League player presented his coach a plaque of recognition.

_____

9. In August the workmen will repair the faulty heating system.

_____

10. The physician canceled all his afternoon appointments.

_____

_____

The following words seem to be associated with one sex. Change each term to a fairer, more generic word.

MANKIND	SEAMSTRESS
CHAIRMAN	HOSTESS
CONGRESSMAN	POLICEMAN
NEWSPAPERMAN	FIREMAN
MAILMAN	WAITRESS

8

COMPOSING THE BUSINESS RESEARCH PAPER

Learning Objectives

Upon completing this chapter, you should be able to:

1. Understand the advantages of using a word processor when writing a business research paper.
2. Engage in all prewriting activities including the constructing of an outline.
3. Write the first draft.
4. Revise and edit the final draft.
5. Explain the guidelines for effective presentation of visual aids.

8.1 USING THE WORD PROCESSORS

Earlier you learned that modern technology has simplified the research process by creating electronic online information services that locate needed information from databases. Computers store the notes generated from the material found in the databases. When you are ready to write, the word processor dramatically changes the act of writing itself. If you are not yet using a word processor, it is in your self-interest to do so, for it is the way of the future. To fully appreciate why this is so, consider the advantages and disadvantages of the word processor. Those few remaining traditionalists who still resist the word processor usually offer the same three reasons that under examination do not stand up well:

1. "I don't know how to use a word processor." Colleges and universities regularly provide instruction on word processor use in workshops or in their computer centers. Writing with a word processor is similar to using a typewriter, but it is more helpful.
2. "I'm afraid I'll push the wrong button and erase all my work." You can protect yourself against accidental loss of material in two ways: (a) at the end of each work session, type the "save" command and print out copies of your work. (b) make a backup disk of your work and store it in a safe place. Also "write protect" the disk so that data cannot be altered or accidentally erased.
3. "I've always typed papers and can't get used to changing to a new tool." All new technology takes time before you become comfortable using it. This obstacle disappears quickly when you discover that the word processor can quickly help you become a more competent and more confident writer. Consider these functions performed by most word processors:

While individual word processing programs vary in levels of sophistication, most standard word processing programs have the ability to add, delete, store, move, and edit text. Because of this capability, the primary benefit of a word processor is that it allows you to insert or delete words, sentences, or paragraphs without retyping the entire draft. When you make any of these changes, the whole text automatically adjusts to the revision. In addition, messy erasures are no longer a problem, because you can make your corrections right on the screen. Another benefit of a word processor is the ability to scroll forward and backward very quickly to review previously written pages.

Some writers make their corrections entirely on the computer screen and print only the final copy. Other writers make changes on the screen, print a copy, then revise with pen or pencil. For most writers, however, making changes on the printed copy is easier than reading a computer screen. After the printed copy is corrected, they go back to the screen and make changes using the "move" command. This change in medium from screen to paper helps the writer find more ways to improve the text.

More will be said about the word processor in the discussion of the three writing stages that follows. Suffice it to say that this new tool gives you greater flexibility and control over the act of writing. This in turn can contribute to the higher quality of the final product. Having acknowledged the contribution that technology can make, you need to remember that the quality of the paper that comes out of the printer is entirely dependent on the quality of the writing that goes into the word processor. To ensure the first half of the "quality in, quality out" maxim, you need to engage in the three stages of the writing process. The key to success is still good writing.

8.2 THE THREE WRITING STAGES

One of the reasons you were asked to make a researcher's schedule (chapter 1) was so you would understand that writing is a process that occurs in stages. To skip one of the stages—a common mistake of the inexperienced writer—is to guarantee that the final product will be less than your best work. While this is true for all writing of any substance it is particularly true for research projects. To be successful you must engage in the same three steps as professional writers: prewriting, writing, and revising.

8.2.1 Prewriting

Prewriting refers to all of the preparatory and organizational activity that precedes the writing of your first draft. Here are some of the prewriting activities already discussed in this text. You may wish to review these sections:

Chapter 1	The Researcher's Journal
	The Researcher's Schedule
Chapter 2	Preparation for Research (entire chapter)
Chapter 3	Searching the Library for Books
	Searching the Library for other sources
Chapter 5	Obtaining Primary Information (entire chapter)
Chapter 6	Reading and Taking Notes (entire chapter)

Once these initial prewriting steps have been completed, making a final plan or working outline remains. This outline serves the same purpose as a road map. It gives you a way to begin and a direction to follow to your final destination. You need a formal plan before you begin to write even though you realize that you may change that plan during each of the next two stages.

8.2.2 Constructing an Outline

When you build an outline for your paper, you first break the paper down into its major parts, specify the subcomponents of each major part, and then arrange those subcomponents in the most logical and coherent sequence. The easiest way to begin your outline is to conceive of your paper as consisting of three major sections: a beginning (introduction), a middle, and an end (see chapter 7). Work on one section at a time, consulting and rearranging your notes as seems most effective. It will become apparent to you which notes are irrelevant, which are usable, and which subjects you may need to further research.

Unless your instructor has certain requirements, the actual format of your outline is up to you. Perhaps the most frequently used system is best:

a. Identify the central idea by writing a thesis or purpose statement.
b. Use Roman numerals (I, II, III) to mark major parts of the paper.
c. Use capital letters (A, B, C) to mark subtopics of one or more paragraphs.
d. Use arabic numbers (1, 2, 3) to mark supporting evidence within minor subtopics.
e. Small letters (a, b, c) mark minor details within supporting evidence.

The actual outline entries may be either full sentences or fragmentary phrases. What matters is that you are clear and consistent. Study the outline that follows. It is taken from the sample paper in chapter 10, entitled *Starting A Successful Catering Business.*

Thesis or Purpose: A combination of dedication, proper market research, and a thorough knowledge of the food and beverage business will ensure the success of your new catering business.

I   Introduction
II   Characteristics of a Caterer
        A. Evaluating your qualifications
        B. Determining your financial position
        C. Making the time commitment
III   Preliminary Market Research
        A. Analyzing the community
        B. Analyzing the catering potential
IV   Deciding What Services to Offer
        A. On-premises catering
        B. Off-premises catering
        C. In-home catering
V   Marketing Your Business
        A. What is marketing?
        B. Basics of marketing
        C. Creating a market
        D. Effective advertising
VI   Financial and Legal Considerations
        A. Hiring a lawyer
        B. Hiring an accountant
VII   Setting Prices
        A. Determining food costs
        B. Determining labor costs
        C. Determining operating costs

D. Deciding desired profit
VIII   Using Package Plans
A. Increasing sales
B. Attracting Customers
IX   Budgeting and the Shakedown Period
X   Conclusion

8.2.3 Prewriting with the Word Processor

Some writers prefer to use a computer from the prewriting stage to the final revised manuscript. When you begin your prewriting, work with a word processor, create a file and name it "prewrite." This is the planning stage when you allow ideas to spontaneously flow into words, sentences, and paragraphs. The word processor encourages speed and continuity that no other writing method allows. Get all of your brainstorming thoughts into the computer without stopping to edit. Some computer users choose to dim the screen so that seeing errors in punctuation and grammar, very common during prewriting, does not interfere with the writer's creative flow of ideas. When most of your prewriting is complete, print out a copy and examine it, making comments with pen or highlighter. These handwritten notations will help you as you continue to write your paper at another stage.

If you are fortunate enough to own a portable (laptop) computer, you can take it along with you to the library and create a "bibliog" file, building a list of alphabetized references. This file, with author, title, and publishing data will be stored until you prepare the "works-cited" page of your paper. At any time you may add new sources and delete old ones from your file. It is important that you enter the information accurately the first time to avoid repeated trips to the library to recover missing pieces of a reference.

You may save time by writing your notes into the word processor. Be sure to create a separate "notes" file for each of your sources and identify each one by name. Include quotation, summary, and paraphrase notes, and store the files. When later drafting the paper, you can retrieve your notes, retaining what you need and deleting the rest. Then merge the usable information from the "notes" file with the text you are writing.

Outlining programs allow you to write a list of topics or subtopics. You may add lines between entries and expand your outline from major divisions to subdivisions and then to supporting details. Easy resequencing is a major feature of these programs.

8.3 WRITING THE FIRST DRAFT

With your outline firmly established, you are ready to begin the first draft. The success of this second stage will depend almost entirely on the quality of your work in the prewriting stage. If you are clear about your topic and have narrowed it, if you are certain of your thesis/

purpose, if you have gathered and arranged sufficient information from all available sources, if you have made an outline—then and only then are you ready to write.

Choose a regular time and place that will enhance your writing. Ideally, such a place will be quiet, free from interruptions and distractions. Be sure you have the necessary equipment, word processor, pens, pencils, and paper. Arrange your notes and outline and begin writing.

It is at this critical point that the student writer can once again benefit from the accumulated experience of professional writers. The way to write a first draft is to write quickly, fully aware that much of what you are writing will be revised and changed in the next stage. This is not the time to edit. This is the time to let the words and ideas flow, without concern for spelling, grammar, sentence structures, or other points of style. If you come up blank in a section, leave it, continue writing, and return to it later.

In his book *A WRITER TEACHES WRITING*, Donald Murray is emphatic about this point:

> The professional writer must be an effective critic of his own writing, but for the first draft he must suspend his ruthless eye. He must find some way to put aside his good, sharp, critical judgment and write a draft, as hard and as fast as possible. . . . When he writes he discovers the holes in his arguments, the logical steps which are passed over, the sentences which grow tangled upon themselves, the paragraphs which collapse, the words which are inadequate, but still he must push on through the first draft. He cannot allow himself to be discouraged at this stage, or to be too critical. The happy accidents will be matched by the misfortunes but still he must complete this piece of writing. He must achieve his destination. (Murray, 121)

Take Donald Murray's advice and push on to the completion of your first draft. Then pause and put some time—at least twenty-four hours—between the first and final draft. This time away from your writing is very helpful. It allows you to bring a fresh perspective to your paper so that you are ready to move to the last stage of revising and editing your business research/paper.

8.4 REVISING AND EDITING THE FINAL DRAFT

After a suitable time, you are ready to rewrite and edit your research paper until it represents your best work. It is time to do all those things that would only have slowed down the writing stage when you were letting the words flow. Successful rewriting requires you to follow a system in order to transform that rough first draft into a carefully crafted final product. One way to begin this third stage is to use a checklist that reflects the ideas you learned in chapter 7 of this book. Read over your manuscript. Check the following points and make the required changes on the word processor or the manuscript itself.

8.4.1 Editing Checklist

WORDS
1. Have I used natural vocabulary that contributes to clarity?
2. Have I used too many words to say what I want to say?
3. Have I used cliches and/or jargon?
4. Have I used specific, concrete words instead of abstract, general language?

SENTENCES
1. Have I started most of my sentences with the subject, followed shortly by the verb?
2. Have I written simple and compound sentences rather than long complex or compound-complex sentences?
3. Have I blended my sentences for variety and rhythm?

PARAGRAPHS
1. Have I used paragraphs when they were needed?
2. Have I constructed paragraphs with topic sentences, supporting sentences, and concluding or transitional sentence?
3. Have I written paragraphs that are both unified and coherent.

ORGANIZATION OF RESEARCH PAPER
1. Have I written an essay which has three-part construction; that is, does it have a beginning, a middle, and an end?

FINAL EDITING
The final step is to proofread for spelling, grammar, and punctuation errors. If you are not using a word processor, you should use a dictionary to find the correct spelling of every word you are uncertain of; consult an English handbook for points of grammar and punctuation. Use these helpful proofreading symbols as you correct your writing.

8.4.2 Proofreading Symbols
When your final draft is typed ask someone else to proofread it. See symbols and correct form on page 118. If you use a word processor, your editing job can be simplified.

8.4.3 Editing Programs on a Word Processor

SPELLING CHECK PROGRAMS
Spelling check programs for computers have dictionaries containing thousands of words to help you find typographical errors and misspelled words. With some programs the misspelled words are highlighted and you can correct them immediately. In some programs the spell check program can display correctly spelled alternative words for you and automatically replace the incorrect word. You must be careful because

Symbol	Meaning	Error	Correction
℘	delete	research ℘ topic	research topic
⌒	close up space	re ⌒ search paper	research paper
Stet.....	ignore correction	proofread the ~~final~~ draft Stet	proofread the final draft
Sp	spell out	locate ③ sources Sp	locate three sources
∪ or tr	transpose	(paper research) tr (paper research)	research paper research paper
¶	new paragraph	¶ The draft is ready	The draft is ready
no ¶	no new paragraph	no ¶ The draft is ready	The draft is ready
cap	capitalize	business research papers cap	Business Research Papers
lc	lower case	Topic Outline lc	topic outline
[	move left	[using the library	using the library
]	move right	] using the library	using the library
_____ Ital	underline or italicize	The New York Times	The New York Times
#	insert space	research#paper	research paper
⋏	insert period	Choose a topic⋏	Choose a topic.
⋏	insert comma	Choose a topic⋏	Choose a topic,
] [	center	] Research paper [	Research paper
5	indent 5 spaces	5 Begin the outline	Begin the outline
ss [	single space between lines	ss [The draft is ready. Type a copy.	The draft is ready. Type a copy.
ds [	double space between lines	ds [The draft is ready. Type a copy.	The draft is ready. Type a copy.
℘	change words	choose ℘ ~~Select~~ a topic.	Choose a topic.

spelling checkers do not pick up all errors. For example, the misuse of *their*, *there*, and *they're* will not be detected by the spell check program. If you used *there* when you meant *their*, the spell checker would not identify the error. It only recognizes the word that is misspelled.

THESAURUS PROGRAMS

Thesaurus programs help you with choosing the appropriate words as you write your paper. A display shows many synonyms (words with similar meaning) and antonyms (words with opposite meaning). You can choose the word that best serves your needs. The electronic thesaurus is a wonderful writing tool, as it allows you to insert the better word right at the keyboard.

STYLE CHECKING PROGRAMS

Style checking programs help you find faulty sentence structure, wordy phrases, sexist language, and errors in punctuation. These programs have limitations. Always understand the context of your writing before you accept the correction of the style checker.

8.5 GUIDELINES FOR EFFECTIVE PRESENTATION OF VISUAL AIDS

TABLES AND FIGURES

Presenting business information in tables and figures conveys the message more effectively than just writing about it in the text of your paper. The old adage "One picture is worth a thousand words" conveys that graphics as well as words communicate ideas to the reader. Computer graphic programs are available that are simple to follow. These programs enable the writer to integrate visual graphs into the writing process. For example, complex numerical data put into understandable illustrations can show the growth or decline of a company or business.

Use a table to communicate statistical information that compares and contrasts data. Any graphic that is not a table, such as graphs, diagrams, and other types of illustrations are considered figures. Each kind of illustration should be numbered consecutively throughout the paper with Arabic numerals (*Table 1, Table 2; Figure 1, Figure 2*, etc.). The captions below the table or figure should indicate the source of information.

Before deciding to use illustrations, ask yourself these questions:

1. Will the illustrations duplicate information in the text? Include an illustration only if it complements the text or eliminates unclear discussion about the data.
2. What idea do you wish to convey to the reader?
3. What type of illustration will be most useful to briefly convey the information?

Types of Illustrations

8.5.1 Tables

A table is organized very much like an outline presenting information in parallel form with a title, main divisions, and subdivisions. The data is clear, concise, and easy to identify.

U.S. Share of Japan's Auto Imports

	Chrysler*	All Imports	Total Auto Sales In Japan (In millions)
1985	51	50,172	3.1
1986	59	68,357	3.2
1987	131	97,750	3.3
1988	174	133,583	3.7
1989	922	180,424	4.2

*Not including Jeeps
Sources: Japan Automobile Importers Association;
Japan Automobile Manufacturers Association

8.5.2 Column Graphs

A column graph is helpful when the reader must compare one item with another, or note one item that changed over a period of time. For example, use a column graph to mark the average selling price of a single-family house in Rhode Island from 1980 to 1989.

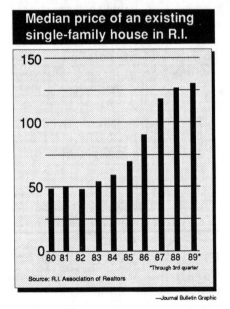

Median price of an existing single-family house in R.I.

*Through 3rd quarter

Source: R.I. Association of Realtors

—Journal Bulletin Graphic

8.5.3 Pie Graphs

The individual slices of the pie represent proportions that make up 100 percent. For example, if you want to illustrate how much money Japan has invested overseas for a given period, each segment would symbolize a different country.

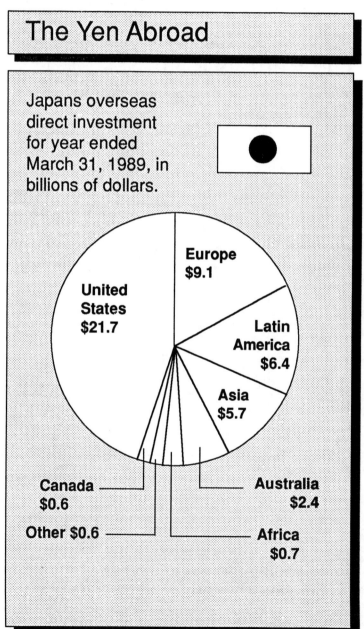

The Yen Abroad

Japans overseas direct investment for year ended March 31, 1989, in billions of dollars.

United States $21.7

Europe $9.1

Latin America $6.4

Asia $5.7

Canada $0.6

Australia $2.4

Other $0.6

Africa $0.7

8.5.4 Line Graphs

A line graph usually shows continuous change in time. Information is plotted on the horizontal (or *X*) axis and on the vertical (or *Y*) axis. For example, use a line graph to represent fluctuations in the number of households viewing the Super Bowl as measured by the Nielsen ratings over a period of twenty years.

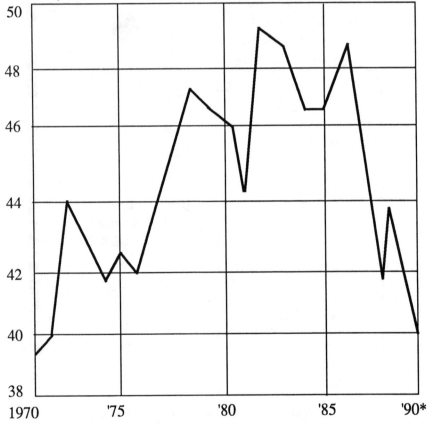

The Ratings Rout
Super Bowl ratings; one point represents
904,000 households

*Preliminary, based on data fom 23 major cities
in which Nielsen uses meters to measure TV viewing
Source: Nielsen Media Research

Application Activities

1. The first word in each entry is spelled correctly. See how quickly you can spot a misspelled word. Read each word,, locating the misspelled words. Use your proofreading symbols.

a. amortize	amortize	ammortize	amortize
b. annuitant	annuitant	anuitant	annuitant
c. bankruptcy	bankruptcy	bankruptcy	bankrupcy
d. proprietorship	propreitorship	proprietorship	proprietorshop
e. nepotism	nepitism	nepotism	nepotism
f. entrepreneur	entrepreneur	enterpreneur	entrepreneur
g. depreciation	depreciation	deprecation	depreciation
h. inventory	invntory	inventory	inventory
i. fiduciary	fiduciary	fiduciary	fiducairy
j. communicate	communicate	communicate	comunicate

2. Use the editing checklist on page 117 to locate errors in spelling, capitalization, punctuation, and sentence fragments. As you correct the following paragraphs, use your proofreading symbols to help you mark the error. The passage is from an article that appeared in *The Wall Street Journal* written by Marcus W. Brauchli.

In recent weeks, many U.S. analysts have warned that major japenese investors might sell off foriegn stocks, and bonds to cover giant losses from a steep tumble on japans own bond market fears of Japanese selling have contributed to the U.S. stockmarket decline. Japaneses bond prices this month have suffered thier steepest drop in half a decade. With many investor's facing a march 31 fiscal year end. Some analysts have suggested, Japanese life insurance companys, trust banks, and securitys firms might try to soften the impact by takeing profits on stocks and bonds abroad, especially in the U.S.

9
DOCUMENTING
BUSINESS SOURCES

Learning Objectives

Upon completing this chapter you should be able to:

1. Recognize the need for documenting sources of information.
2. Prepare an in-text parenthetical note following the MLA and APA styles.
3. Prepare a works cited list according to MLA style.
4. Prepare a references list according to APA style.
5. Document sources following the Notes style.

9.1 MLA DOCUMENTATION

Most college courses in the humanities require papers to follow the author-page documentation style of the Modern Language Association (MLA). The following section presents examples of the many sources you will need to use in writing a business research paper. If you should need a more extensive discussion of the MLA style, consult the *MLA Handbook for Writers of Research Papers*, third edition, edited by Joseph Gibaldi and Walter S. Achtert, 1988.

The two basic steps of MLA documentation are:

A. Preparing the parenthetical note within the body of the paper, citing the source of material by giving the author's name and the page number between parentheses. No comma is used to separate name and page number.

```
(Freeman, Frederickson, and Miller 75-80.)
(Graziano 41)
(Porter 88)
```

B. Preparing the works-cited entry, an alphabetical listing at the end, of all sources used in the paper.

```
                    Works Cited


Freeman, Caryl, Esther Frederickson, and Joanne Miller.
     Support Staff Procedures in the Electronic Office.
     Englewood, NJ: Prentice, 1986.
Graziano, Loretta.  Interpreting the Money Supply: Human
     and Institutional Factors.  New York: Quorum, 1987.
Porter, Sylvia.  Love and Money.  New York: Morrow, 1985.
```

9.1.1 Preparing the Parenthetical Note

MLA recommends a concise, clear, and accurate system for citing an extensive variety of sources. The following are models of the typical MLA parenthetical citation. The source is then given as it would appear in a works-cited list.

1. Cite the author's last name and the page number(s) between parentheses.

```
     One researcher observes that teamwork involves
cooperative employees who will strive for a common work
goal (Waterman 207).
```

Place the note at the end of your sentence, before the final mark of punctuation. Notice that there is no comma between the author's name and the page number(s). Type a single space to separate name and page number(s). The page number is not preceded by p. or pp.

2. Use the author's name in your sentence, and provide only the page number(s) in parentheses.

```
     According to Waterman teamwork involves co-operative
employees who will strive for a common goal (207).
```

```
                    Works Cited


Waterman, Robert.  The Renewal Factor: How the Best Get
     and Keep the Competitive Edge.  Toronto: Bantam,
     1987.
```

3. For a direct quotation use the last name of the author in your sentence and place page numbers at the end of the quotation.

In a discussion on the causes of organizational change, Bridges said, "This leads to a speculator mentality among organizational leaders and fuels today's brisk market in merger and acquisitions" (12).

Or for a direct quotation do not use last name of author in your sentence. Instead place last name of author and page number in parentheses at the end of the quotation.

"This leads to a speculator mentality among organizational leaders and fuels today's brisk market in merger and acquisitions" (Bridges 12).

Works Cited

Bridges, William. <u>Surviving Corporate Transition:</u>
<u>Rational Management in a World of Mergers, Layoffs,</u>
<u>Start-Ups, Takeovers, Divestitures, Deregulations,</u>
<u>and New Technologies</u>. New York: Doubleday, 1988.

4. Place the parenthetical note after the end punctuation if the cited passage is a lengthy direct quotation. (For quotations more than four lines long, indent ten spaces from the left margin, double-spaced and without quotation marks.)
Effective listening is the key to successful leadership, as one manager explains:

There's an important emotional component to this. There's listening, and then there's engaged listening. The note-taking habit is a tip-off to the latter, but there's more to it than that. Engaged listening may be the principal mark of concern that one human being can evince for another in any setting (Peters 437).

Works Cited

Peters, Tom. <u>Thriving on Chaos: Handbook for a</u>
<u>Management Revolution</u>. New York: Knopf, 1987.

5. To cite sources within a single sentence, place each note after the statements each supports.

Waterman asserts the importance of visible management attention to motivate employees (11), and Peters adds effective management as a component of visible management (435).

6. Do not repeat the author's name in second or subsequent references to the sources, unless a different reference intervenes.

Lawrence G. Chait examines some computer systems capable of performing intelligent human activities that involve language, learning, and problem solving (54). Some of the most recent developments in this area are already a marketplace reality. Artificial intelligence, he believes, will expand our capabilities in all fields of human endeavor (56). Even the areas of machine vision and natural language for databases have been cited as the products of artificial intelligence research (Kinnucan 17). For example, according to Chait artificial intelligence will allow noncomputer experts to communicate with their computers using everyday language (54).

Works Cited

Chait, Lawrence G. "Direct Marketing in the Epoch of
     Artificial Intelligence." Direct Marketing June
1985: 54-61.

7. If you use more than one work by a single author, use the author's name in your sentence, and add a shortened version of the title of the book to each note, followed by the page number(s). Underline the shortened title.

To Allan Cox, an experienced executive recruiter, "warmth is the appetite for showing and being shown acceptance" (Making of Achiever 9). At the corporate level an atmosphere of warmth promotes a feeling of acceptance. Cox asserts that "the inter-personal network" must be as solid as the ties that bind a family, neighborhood, or religious institute (Achiever's Profile 68).

Works Cited

Cox, Allan. The Achiever's Profile: One Hundred
       Questions and Answers to Sharpen Your Executive
       Instincts. New York: Amacon, 1988.
- - -. The Making of the Achiever: How to Win Distinction
       in Your Company. New York: Dodd, 1985.

8. When citing a work with no author, list a shortened version of the title followed by the page number. Begin the shortened title with the first word of the full title (excluding *A, An, The*) so that the correct citation can be found. For example, an unsigned magazine article entitled "Public Service Ads Top $1 Billion in '87" might be shortened to "Public Service." Capitalize all significant words of the shortened title of the article. Put quotation marks around shortened title.

("Public Service" 72)

Works Cited

"Public Service Ads Top $1 Billion in '87."
       Advertising Age 6 June 1988: 72.

9. When citing a book by two or three authors, you may name two or three authors in your sentence or in a parenthetical note. When citing a book by more than three authors, name the first author followed by et al., the Latin expression for "and others."

Doerflinger and Rivkin agree that the era of computers, telecommunications, biotechnology, and space technologies are evidence of another Industrial Revolution (7).

Following the Civil War period, the Industrial Revolution expanded the need for farming and textile products in America (Sandage, Fryburger, and Rotzoll 25).

Aaron et al. stress the possibility that welfare payments may in the long run, "perpetuate poverty,

especially among female headed families in inner cities"
(74-75).

Works Cited

Aaron, Henry J., et al. <u>Economic Choices</u>: 1987.
     Washington: Brookings Institute, 1986.
Doerflinger, Thomas M., and Jack L. Rivkin. <u>Risks and</u>
     <u>Reward: Venture Capital and the Making of America's</u>
     <u>Great Industries</u>. New York: Random, 1987.
Sandage, C.H., Vernon Fryburger, and Kim Rotzoll.
     <u>Advertising: Theory and Practice</u>. New York: Longman,
     1989.

10. To cite a work by a corporate author, integrate the information
with your sentence. For clarity it would be better to name the corporate
author in your sentence and place only page number(s) in parentheses.

American Telephone and Telegraph's Annual Report for
1988 announced a new European mobile phone system to meet
motorists' needs (13).

Works Cited

American Telephone and Telegraph. <u>Annual Report</u>.
     AT&T, 1988.

11. To cite one volume from a multivolume work, indicate in the
parenthetical reference the specific volume used, followed by two
spaces and the page(s). Do not use the word "vol."

John Maynard Keynes asserts that theater and arts
exist for public and not for private purposes (Moggridge
28: 354-55).

Works Cited

Moggridge, Donald, ed. <u>The Collected Writings of John</u>
     <u>Maynard Keynes</u>. 30 vols. London: Macmillan, 1982.

12. To cite more than one work in a single parenthetical reference,
cite each work as you normally would in a reference, but use semi-
colons to separate the citations.

(Shamoon 43; Sahgal and Crawford 37)

(Lowry, Weinrich, and Steade 87; Crosby 55)

Works Cited

Crosby, Philip B. <u>Running Things: The Art of Making
    Things Happen</u>. New York: McGraw, 1986.

Lowry, James. R., Bernard W. Weinrich, and Richard D.
    Steade. <u>Business in Today's World</u>. Cincinnati:
    South-Western, 1990.

Sahgal, Pavan, and Diane Crawford. "The New Moguls of
    Computerized Investing." <u>Wall Street Computer
    Review</u> Mar. 1985: 35-48.

Shamoon, Sherrie. "The Bank is a True Believer in Slick
    Slides and Charts." <u>Management Technology</u> Dec.
    1984: 42-54.

9.1.2 Preparing the Works Cited List

In writing your research paper you will borrow material from a variety of books, periodicals, journals, and nonprint sources. To avoid plagiarism you are obligated to indicate where you found the borrowed facts, opinions, or quotations. The MLA style of documentation recommends that you acknowledge your sources by keying references in the text to a works-cited list at the end of your research paper. The works-cited list simplifies documentation because it includes all of the wide variety of sources used in your paper.

Follow these general MLA guidelines to prepare the list of works cited.

1. Begin the works cited list on its own page following the body of the research paper. If the conclusion of your paper appears on page 10, the works cited list will appear on page 11.

2. Begin the first line of each entry flush with the left margin, and indent the subsequent line or lines five spaces from the left margin. Double space between successive lines of an entry and between entries.

Lu, David J. <u>Inside Corporate Japan: The Art of
    Fumble-Free Management</u>. Cambridge: Productivity,
    1987.

Ming, Zhang. "Beijing Continues to Open the Door."
    <u>Beijing Review</u> 24 July 1989: 19-20.

Quinn, Jane Bryant. <u>Everyone's Money Book</u> New York:
    Delacourt, 1979.

3. Alphabetize entries according to author's last name. Reverse author's name, adding a comma after the last name. Give the author's name as it appears on the title page. Use initials if the title page does. Never abbreviate a name given in full. Exclude titles and degrees of authors.

```
Gasteneau, Gary L.

Stigum, Marcia.

Tewles, Richard J. and Edward S. Brady.
```

4. To list more than one work by the same author, give the name in the first reference only. Thereafter, in place of the author's name type three hyphens and a period, skip two spaces, and write the title. Alphabetize the works according to title (excluding the articles *A*, *An*, *The*).

```
Friedman, Milton.  Dollars and Deficits: Living with
     America's Economic Problems.  Englewood Cliffs, NJ:
     Prentice, 1968.
- - -.  Money and Economic Development.  New York: Praeger,
     1973.
- - -.  The Optimum Quantity of Money and Other Essays.
     Chicago: Aldine, 1969.
- - -.  There's No Such Thing as a Free Lunch.  La Salle,
     IL: Open Court, 1975.
```

5. To ensure completeness type a continuous line under the entire title of a book. Capitalize all significant words in the title. Place a period at the end of the title. Do not underline the period.

```
Start Up Telemarketing: How to Launch a Profitable
     Sales Operation.
Unnecessary Choices: The Hidden Life of the
     Executive Woman.
Tax Planning for Acquisitions in the United States.
```

6. Underline the titles of books, plays, films, pamphlets, and periodicals. Drop the article *The* from the names of newspapers.

```
Making Accounting Policy: The Quest for Credibility in
     Financial Reporting
Death of a Salesman
Wall Street
How to Run Effective Meetings
Black Enterprise
```

<u>Christian Science Monitor</u>

<u>Boston Globe</u>

7. Place quotation marks around titles of articles appearing in newspapers and periodicals. End the article with a period before the closing quotation mark.

"Consumers in 1988: The Year in Review."

"Family Carries on Booming Business."

"The Next Generation."

"The Handicapped Make Headway on Madison Avenue."

8. Underline a title of a book when it occurs within a title between quotation marks.

"Comer: <u>Nation of Strangers</u> Hinders Education."

9. Place quotation marks around titles of shorter works that appear in larger works.

Neugarten, Bernice. "Acting One's Age: New Rules for
    Old." <u>The Elderly Market Selected Readings</u>.
    Ed.Charles D. Schewe. Chicago: AMA, 1985.

10. Place a period followed by two spaces after author and title.

Suzaki, Kiyoshi. <u>The New Manufacturing Challenge:</u>
    <u>Techniques for Continuous Improvement</u>.

Jennings, Diane. <u>Self-Made Women: Twelve of America's</u>
    <u>Leading Entrepreneurs Talk About Success, Self-</u>
    <u>Image, and the Superwoman</u>.

11. Use a colon to separate volume and year of periodical from the page numbers.

Gersick, Connie J.G. "Marking Time: Predictable
    Transitions in Task Groups." <u>Academy of Management</u>
    <u>Journal</u> 32 (1989): 274-309.

12. For page numbers through 99, give the second number in full (4–5, 12–15, 36–52, 87–99).

Harding, Philip A. "The New Technologies for Consumer
    Policy." <u>Consumerism and Beyond: Research</u>
    <u>Perspectives on the Future Social Environment</u>. Ed.
    Paul N. Bloom. Cambridge: Marketing Science
    Institute, 1982. 82-84.

For page numbers larger than 99, give only the last two digits of the second number unless more are necessary (98–103, 104–06, 245–67).

```
Krugman, H.E.  "The Impact of Television Advertising:
     Learning Without Involvement."  Public Opinion
     Quarterly 29 (1965): 349-56.
```

13. When an article is not printed on consecutive pages, write only the first page number and a plus sign. The plus sign means the article appears on discontinuous pages. In this example the unsigned article is written on pages 66, 68, and 73.

```
"How Cosmetics Makers are Touching Up Their Strategies."
     Business Week 23 Sept 1985: 66+.
```

MLA GUIDE: CITING BOOKS

The numbered list that follows will help you locate the type of source you will need to cite your reference. On the pages that follow you will find examples of works-cited entries and parenthetical notes for each type of source on the list.

1. Book by one author, p. 135
2. Book by two or three authors, pp. 135–136
3. Book by more than three authors, p. 136
4. Book by two authors with same last name, p. 136
5. Two or more books by same author, pp. 136–137
6. Book with collaborator, p. 137
7. Book by a corporate author, p. 137
8. Book by anonymous author, p. 137
9. Book with editor or compiler, p. 138
10. Book with author and editor, p. 138
11. Book with publisher's imprint, p. 138
12. Anthology or compilation, p. 139
13. Work in an anthology, p. 139
14. Introduction, preface, foreword, afterword, pp. 139–140
15. Multivolume work, p. 140
16. Edition other than the first, pp. 140–141
17. Book in a series, p. 141
18. Republished book, p. 141
19. Published proceedings of a conference, p. 141
20. Translation, pp. 141–142
21. Book published before 1900, p. 142
22. A pamphlet, p. 142
23. Government publication, p. 142

24. Article in a reference work, pp. 142–143
25. Book in a language other than English, p. 143

MLA Documentation
Citing Books: Arrangement of Required Information

An entry in a list of works cited has three main divisions: 1. author's name followed by a period and two spaces, 2. title of book followed by period and two spaces, 3. place of publication followed by colon and one space, publisher, and date.

Biggart, Nicole Woolsey. Charismatic Capitalism: Direct
    Selling Organizations in America. Chicago: U of
    Chicago P, 1989.

1. Author's name:

Biggart, Nicole Woolsey.

2. Title of book:

Charismatic Capitalism Direct Selling Organizations in
    America.

3. Place of publication:

Chicago:

4. Name of publisher:

U of Chicago P,

5. Date of publication:

1989.

1. MLA: BOOK BY ONE AUTHOR

WORKS CITED FORM:

Fantetti, Donna J. Career Directions: Special Edition.
    Providence: P.A.R., 1987.

PARENTHETICAL NOTE:

(Fantetti 86)

2. MLA: BOOK BY TWO OR THREE AUTHORS

Give the names of the authors in the order in which they appear on the title page. Reverse only the name of the first author. Add a comma and give the other name(s) in normal order.

WORKS CITED FORM:

Hardesty, Sarah, and Nehama Jacobs. <u>The Crisis of Women</u>
     <u>in Corporate America</u>. New York: Franklin Watts,
     1986.

PARENTHETICAL NOTE:

(Hardesty and Jacobs 67-77)

WORKS CITED FORM:

Urban, Glen L., John R. Hauser, and Nikhilesh Dholakia.
     <u>Essentials of New Product Management</u>. Englewood
     Cliffs, NJ: Prentice, 1987.

Note: If the city is unfamiliar, add the state for clarity.

PARENTHETICAL NOTE:

(Urban, Hauser, and Dholakia 44-49)

3. MLA: BOOK BY MORE THAN THREE AUTHORS

You may name only the first author and add et al. ("and others"), or
you may give all names in full in the order in which they appear on
the title page.

WORKS CITED FORM:

Aaron, Henry J., et al. <u>Economic Choices 1987</u>.
     Washington: Brookings, 1986.

PARENTHETICAL NOTE:

(Aaron et al. 67)

4. MLA: BOOK BY TWO AUTHORS WITH SAME LAST NAME

WORKS CITED FORM:

Lott, Catherine S., and Oscar C. Lott. <u>How to Land a</u>
     <u>Better Job</u>. Lincolnwood: VGM Career Horizons, 1985.

PARENTHETICAL NOTE:

(Lott and Lott 78-82)

5. MLA TWO OR MORE BOOKS BY SAME AUTHOR

WORKS CITED FORM:

Drucker, Peter F. <u>The Changing World of the Executive</u>.
     New York: Times, 1982.

- - -.   <u>Management: Tasks, Responsibilities, Practices</u>.
New York: Harper, 1974.
- - -.   <u>Managing for Results</u>. New York: Harper, 1964.

PARENTHETICAL NOTE:

(Drucker 22-23)

6. MLA: BOOK WITH COLLABORATOR

Begin the entry with the author's name followed by a comma. Add *with* and the name of the collaborator.

WORKS CITED FORM:

Cunningham, Mary, with Fran Schumer. <u>Powerplay: What</u>
<u>Really Happened at Bendix</u>. New York: Linden-Simon,
1984.

PARENTHETICAL NOTE:

(Cunningham 86-90)

7. MLA: BOOK BY A CORPORATE AUTHOR

A corporate author may be a group whose individual members are not identified on the title page. Cite the book by the corporate author even if the corporate author is the publisher of the book.

WORKS CITED FORM:

Business Research Services, Inc. <u>National Directory of</u>
<u>Minority-owned Firms</u>. Lombard, IL: BRS, 1986.

PARENTHETICAL NOTE:

(Business Research 56)

8. MLA: BOOK BY ANONYMOUS AUTHOR

If the book has no author's name on the title page, begin the entry with the title of the book.

WORKS CITED FORM:

<u>Women Helping Women: A State-by-State Directory of</u>
<u>Services</u>   New York: Women's Action Alliance, 1981.

PARENTHETICAL NOTE:

(Women Helping Women 49)

9. MLA: BOOK WITH EDITOR OR COMPILER

Begin the entry with the name of the editor or editors. Place a comma before *ed.* or *eds.* (lower case).

WORKS CITED FORM:

Goodwin, Geoffry, and James Mayall, eds.   A New
    International Commodity Regime.   New York: St.
    Martin's, 1980.

PARENTHETICAL NOTE:

(Goodwin and Mayall 27-45)

WORKS CITED FORM:

Andriole, Stephen J., ed.   Corporate Crisis Management.
    Princeton: Petrocelli, 1985.

PARENTHETICAL NOTE:

(Andriole 36-45)

10. MLA: BOOK WITH AUTHOR AND EDITOR

Write the author's name and the title of book. After the title write *Ed.* followed by the name of the editor.

WORKS CITED FORM:

Galbraith, John Kenneth.   Economics and Laughter.   Ed.
    Andrea D. Williams.   Boston: Houghton, 1971.

PARENTHETICAL NOTE:

(Galbraith 98)

11. MLA: PUBLISHER'S IMPRINT

An imprint identifies the many groups of books of a publisher. When you cite a book under an imprint, give the name of the imprint followed by a hyphen and the name of the publisher: Anchor-Doubleday, Camelot-Avon, and Linden-Simon.

WORKS CITED FORM:

Gardenswartz, Lee, and Anita Rowe.   What It Takes: Good
    News from 100 of America's Top Professional and
    Business Women.   New York: Dolphin-Doubleday, 1987.

PARENTHETICAL NOTE:

(Gardenswartz and Rowe 79-88)

12. MLA: ANTHOLOGY OR COMPILATION

Begin with the name of the editor or compiler followed by a comma, a space, and *ed.* or *comp.*

WORKS CITED FORM:

Brymer, Robert A., ed. Introduction to Hotel and
Restaurant Management. 5th ed. Dubuque:
Kendall-Hunt, 1988.

PARENTHETICAL NOTE:

(Brymer 73)

13. MLA: WORK IN AN ANTHOLOGY

State the author's name and title of the article you are citing. Enclose the title in quotation marks. Underline the title of the anthology. After the title write *Ed.* and give the editor's name.

NOTE: Cite the inclusive pages for the piece at the end of the citation, after the year of publication, a period, and two spaces.

WORKS CITED FORM:

Cooper, Caroline A. "Careers in the Hospitality
Industry." Introduction to Hotel and Restaurant
Management. Ed. Robert A. Brymer. 5th ed.
Dubuque: Kendall-Hunt, 1988. 26-34.

PARENTHETICAL NOTE:

(Cooper 26-34)

14. MLA: INTRODUCTION, PREFACE, FOREWORD, AFTERWORD

To cite information from an introduction, a preface, a foreword, or an afterword, begin with the name of its author, then identify the part being cited. Capitalize the identified part. If the writer of the "part" is also the author of the complete work, use only the last name after *By.* If the writer of the part is different from the author of the complete work, cite the author of the work after the title. Give the full name, in normal order, preceded by the word *By.*

WORKS CITED FORM:

Nivens, Beatryce. Introduction. The Black Woman's
Career Guide. By Nivens. New York: Anchor-
Doubleday, 1982. xii-xiv.

PARENTHETICAL NOTE:

(Nivens xii-xiv)

WORKS CITED FORM:

Blanchard, Kenneth.   Foreword.   Swim with the Sharks
      Without Being Eaten Alive: Outsell, Outmanage, and
      Outnegotiate Your Competition.   By Harvey Mackey.
      New York: Morrow, 1988.

PARENTHETICAL NOTE:

(Blanchard 7-10)

WORKS CITED FORM:

Hamlin, Sonya.   Afterword.   How to Talk So People Listen:
      The Real Key to Job Success.   By Hamlin.   New York:
      Harper, 1988.   257-58.

PARENTHETICAL NOTE:

(Hamlin 257-58)

15. MLA: MULTIVOLUME WORK

When you have used two or more volumes of a multivolume work, give the total number of volumes (8 vols.) in the work. Place this information between the title and the publication information. Place specific references to volume and page numbers (4 : 37-48) in the parenthetical note.

WORKS CITED:

Greenstein, Fred I. and Nelson W. Polsby, eds.   Political
      Science: Scope and Theory.   8 vols.   Reading, MA:
      Addison, 1975.

PARENTHETICAL NOTE:

(Greenstein and Polsby 4: 37-48)

16. MLA: EDITION OTHER THAN THE FIRST

The title page will indicate the edition of the book. A book that gives no edition number on its title page is probably a first edition. You need not indicate a first edition in your bibliography. If, however, you are using an edition other than the first edition, identify it in your entry as follows: (2nd ed., 3rd ed., 4th ed.). When more than one copyright date is listed, cite the latest date.

WORKS CITED FORM:

Shao, Stephen P.   Mathematics for Management and Finance.
      6th ed.   Cincinnati: South-Western, 1991.

PARENTHETICAL NOTE:

(Shao 22)

17. MLA: BOOK IN A SERIES

If the book you are citing is part of a series, include the series name, neither underlined nor enclosed in quotation marks. Include the series number, followed by a period, before the publication information.

WORKS CITED FORM:

Knight, John B., and Charles A. Salter. <u>Food Service</u>
<u>Standards in Resorts</u>. L.J. Minor Foodservice
Standards Ser. 6. New York: CBI-Van Nostrand, 1987.

PARENTHETICAL NOTE:

(Knight and Salter 33-39)

18. MLA: REPUBLISHED BOOK

The original place of publication, publisher, and date of publication may precede the current publication information.

WORKS CITED FORM:

Presnell, L.S., ed. <u>Money and Banking in Japan</u>. Trans.
S. Nishimura. Japan: Bank of Japan, 1969. London:
Macmillan, 1975.

PARENTHETICAL NOTE:

(Presnell 94-102)

19. MLA: PUBLISHED PROCEEDINGS OF A CONFERENCE

WORKS CITED FORM:

Zanot, Eric. "Public Attitudes Toward Advertising."
<u>Advertising in a New Age</u>. Ed. Keith H. Hunt. Proc.
of the Annual Conference of the American Academy of
Advertsing. Provo, UT: American Academy of
Advertising, 1981. 142-46.

PARENTHETICAL NOTE:

(Zanot 142)

20. MLA: TRANSLATION

Give the author's name first. If there is an editor and a translator give both names with abbreviated titles *Trans.* or *Ed.*

WORKS CITED FORM:

Montagne, Prosper. The New Larousse Gastronomique. Ed.
    Charlotte Turgeon. Trans. Marion Hunter. New York:
    Crown, 1977.

PARENTHETICAL NOTE:

(Montagne 36-40)

21. MLA: BOOK PUBLISHED BEFORE 1900

You may omit the name of the publisher. Use a comma instead of a colon after the place of publication.

WORKS CITED FORM:

McVickar, John. Outlines of Political Economy.
    New York, 1825.

PARENTHETICAL NOTE:

(McVickar 72)

22. MLA: A PAMPHLET

Cite a pamphlet as you would a book.

WORKS CITED FORM:

Labor Market Review. Richmond: Virginia Employment
    Commission, 1988.

PARENTHETICAL NOTE:

(Labor 2)

23. MLA: GOVERNMENT PUBLICATION

WORKS CITED FORM:

United States: Office of Consumer Affairs. Consumer's
    Resource Handbook. 4th ed. Washington: GPO, 1988.

PARENTHETICAL NOTE:

To avoid a lengthy note, name the document in the body of the paper.

"This information is based on material from...."

24. MLA: ARTICLE IN A REFERENCE WORK

WORKS CITED FORM:

Gibson, Anne, and Timothy Fast. "Employment." The
    Women's Atlas of the United States. New York: Facts
    on File, 1986.

PARENTHETICAL NOTE:

(Gibson and Fast 31)

25. MLA: BOOK IN A LANGUAGE OTHER THAN ENGLISH

WORKS CITED FORM:

Odaka, Kunio. Nihonteki Keiei: Sono Shinwa to Genjitsu
    <Japanese Management: A Forward Looking Analysis>.
    Tokyo: Chuo Koron-Sha, 1984.

PARENTHETICAL NOTE:

(Odaka 28)

MLA GUIDE: CITING NEWSPAPERS, MAGAZINES AND PERIODICALS

1. Article from newspaper, author named, p. 144
2. Article from newspaper, no author named, p. 144
3. Article from newspaper, different editions, pp. 144–145
4. Article from newspaper, editorial, p. 145
5. Article from weekly or biweekly magazine, p. 145
6. Article from monthly or bimonthly magazine, p. 145
7. Unsigned article from magazine, p. 146
8. Article in a scholarly journal with continuous pagination, p. 146
9. Article in a scholarly journal that pages each issue separately, p. 146
10. Letter to the editor, pp. 146–147
11. A review, p. 147
12. An abstract from *Dissertation Abstracts* or *Dissertation Abstracts International*, p. 147

Citing Periodicals: Arrangement of Required Information

Periodicals include newspapers, magazines, and scholarly journals. An entry for an article in a periodical has four main divisions: (1) author, followed by a period and two spaces; (2) title of article, enclosed in quotation marks (End the article with a period before the closing quotation mark.), two spaces; (3) name of periodical, and (4) publication information. For scholarly journals the publication information includes the journal title, the volume number, the year of publication and the inclusive page numbers of the article.

Bertrand, Kate "Get Ready for Global Capitalism."
    Business Marketing Jan. 1990: 42-44+.

1. Author's name: Bertrand, Kate.
2. Title of the article enclosed in quotation marks: "Get Ready for Global Capitalism."

3. Name of the magazine underlined: <u>Business Marketing</u>
4. Date of publication followed by colon: Jan. 1990:
5. Page(s) of publication: 42-44 +.

Note: When the entire article is not printed on consecutive pages, write only the first and consecutive page numbers followed by a plus sign. The plus sign means that the article is continued on other pages.

```
Sabath, Ann Marie.  "Client Sees Restaurant as an
      Extension of Your Office."  Washington Times 20 June
      1989: E9.
```

1. Author's name: Sabath, Ann Marie.
2. Title of article enclosed in quotation marks: "Client Sees Restaurant as an Extension of Your Office."
3. Name of Newspaper underlined: <u>Washington Times</u>
4. Date of Publication: 20 June 1989:
5. Section and page number of publication : E9. If the newspaper numbers its pages with numbers and letters (B1, E9), indicate the page numbers as they appear on the page.

1. MLA: ARTICLE FROM NEWSPAPER, AUTHOR NAMED

WORKS CITED FORM:

```
Hanafin, Theresa M.  "Marketer Reduces Prices 25% on
      Marlborough Street Condos."  Boston Globe 4
      Jan. 1990: 29+.
```

PARENTHETICAL NOTE:

```
(Hanafin 29)
```

2. MLA: ARTICLE FROM NEWSPAPER, NO AUTHOR NAMED

Put the title of the article in the author position. Alphabetize by the first significant word in the title.

WORKS CITED FORM:

```
"The TV Commercial Tries on Some Disguises."  New York
      Times 1 Sept. 1985: F7.
```

PARENTHETICAL NOTE:

```
("TV Commercial" F7)
```

3. MLA: ARTICLE FROM NEWSPAPER, DIFFERENT EDITION

WORKS CITED FORM:

```
Miller, Michael W.  "A New Picture for Computer Graphics:
      The Next Wave in PC's May Be Use of Video."  Wall
      Street Journal 5 July 1989, eastern ed.: B1.
```

PARENTHETICAL NOTE:

(Miller 1)

4. MLA: ARTICLE FROM NEWSPAPER, EDITORIAL

WORKS CITED FORM:

"Forest Service's Watershed Blitz." <u>Seattle</u>
    <u>Post-Intelligencer</u> 24 Dec. 1989, editorial: E3.

PARENTHETICAL NOTE:

("Forest" E3)

5. MLA: ARTICLE FROM WEEKLY OR BIWEEKLY MAGAZINE

Give the exact date of publication, a colon, the page numbers, and a period.

WORKS CITED FORM:

Saunders, Laura. "Freezing Out the Estate Freeze."
    <u>Forbes</u> 17 Oct. 1988: 80-88.

PARENTHETICAL NOTE:

(Saunders 83)

6. MLA: ARTICLE FROM MONTHLY OR BIMONTHLY MAGAZINE

Give the name of the month and the year. Abbreviate all months except May, June, and July. If an issue is identified by two months, place a hyphen between their abbreviated names.

WORKS CITED FORM:

Lodge, Arthur. "That is the Most You Will Ever Pay."
    <u>Journal of Accountancy</u> Oct. 1985: 44.

PARENTHETICAL NOTE:

(Lodge 44)

WORKS CITED FORM:

Beadle, Carson E. "The Future of Employee Benefits: More
    Mandates Ahead." <u>Compensation and Benefits Review</u>
    Nov.- Dec. 1988: 35-44.

PARENTHETICAL NOTE:

(Beadle 37)

7. MLA: UNSIGNED ARTICLE FROM MAGAZINE

Put the title of the article in the author position. Use a shortened form of the article in the parenthetical note.

WORKS CITED FORM:

"Determining How Ads are Seen." Dun's Business Month
      Feb. 1982: 85-86.

PARENTHETICAL NOTE:

("Determining How" 85-86)

8. MLA: ARTICLE IN A SCHOLARLY JOURNAL WITH CONTINUOUS PAGINATION

If the journal uses continuous pagination throughout the annual volume, then after the title place the volume number, the year of publication in parentheses, a colon, and the page numbers. (For example, when the first issue ends on page 200 and the second issue begins on page 201.) End entry with a period.

WORKS CITED FORM:

Lien, Da-Hsiang Donald.   "Cash Settlement Provisions on
      Futures Contracts." Journal of Futures Markets 9
      (1989): 263-70.

PARENTHETICAL NOTE:

(Lien 263-64)

9. MLA: ARTICLE IN A SCHOLARLY JOURNAL THAT PAGES EACH ISSUE SEPARATELY

Some journals begin each issue with page 1. Give the volume number, a period (without a space after the period), the issue number, the year of publication in parentheses, a colon, and the page numbers.

WORKS CITED FORM:

Burt, David. N.   "Managing Product Quality Through
      Strategic Purchasing." Sloan Management Review 30.3
      (1989): 39-48.

PARENTHETICAL NOTE:

(Burt 39-40)

10. MLA: LETTER TO THE EDITOR

WORKS CITED FORM:

Heller, Lenore I.   Letter. Business Month Nov. 1988: 6.

PARENTHETICAL NOTE:

(Heller 6)

11. MLA: A REVIEW

WORKS CITED FORM:

Liles, Shelley. Rev. of Entrepreneurial Woman. USA
    Today 21 June 1989: B4.

PARENTHETICAL NOTE:

(Liles B4)

12. MLA: AN ABSTRACT FROM *DISSERTATION ABSTRACTS* OR *DISSERTATION ABSTRACTS INTERNATIONAL*

WORKS CITED FORM:

Al-Loughani, Nabeel Essa. "The Impact of Business Groups
    on Domestic Lending: An Investigation of the
    Portfolio Behavior of Commercial Banks in Kuwait."
    DAI 49 (1989): 8818895. Golden Gate U.

PARENTHETICAL NOTE:

(Al-Loughani 45-55)

OTHER SOURCES

Citing Other Sources

1. MLA: COMPUTER SOFTWARE

Give the name of the writer of the program, if there is one. Give the
title of the program, underlined, the version of the program (vers.) and

the identifying label (Computer Software), the distributor, and the year of publication. At the end of the entry add any other pertinent information.

WORKS CITED FORM:

```
dBase III PLUS.  Vers.  1.0.  Computer Software.
     Ashton-Tate, 1986.  IBM/MS-DOS.
```

PARENTHETICAL NOTE:
It is better to name the software in the body of the paper.

2. MLA: MATERIAL FROM A COMPUTER SERVICE

Treat information obtained from a computer service such as Dialog or BRS like other printed material. At the end of the entry cite the name of the service and the identifying number.

WORKS CITED FORM:

```
Grensing, Lin.  "An AA Primer: Eight Tips on Affirmative
     Action."  Management World Jan. 1987: 34-35.  Dialog
     File 75, item 0362837.
```

PARENTHETICAL NOTE:

```
(Grensing 34)
```

3. MLA: TELEVISION AND RADIO PROGRAMS

Include the title of the program, underlined; the director, narrator, producer; the network (PBS); the local station; the city; and the date of broadcast.

WORKS CITED FORM:

```
Wall Street Week.  With Louis Rukeyser. Dir. George
     Benemen.  Prod. John H. Davis, and Rich Dubroff.
     PBS WGBH, Maryland Public Television, Owings Mills,
     5 Jan. 1990
```

PARENTHETICAL NOTE:
It is better to name the program in the text of your paper.

4. MLA: AUDIO RECORDING, VIDEO CASSETTE, FILMSTRIP, FILM

Include the speaker; the title, underlined; the director; the distributor; and the year. Add any pertinent information such as the writers, the performers, and the length of film.

WORKS CITED FORM: AUDIO RECORDING

Nieremberg, Gerard I. Nieremberg on Negotiating. Sound
    Recording. Waco, TX: Success Motivation, 1983.
    51 min.

PARENTHETICAL NOTE:
It would be better to name the recording in the text.

In the audio recording, Nieremberg on Negotiating,
Nieremberg describes skills helpful in persuading people
to reach agreements.

WORKS CITED FORM: VIDEOTAPE

Schoumacher, David. Economics USA: Perfect Competition.
    Video Cassette. Prod. and dir. Lou Barbesh.
    Chicago: Films, Inc. 1986. 28 min.

PARENTHETICAL NOTE:
It would be better to name the video cassette in the text.

In the video cassette, Economics USA: Perfect
Competition, Schoumacher illustrates the concepts of
competition, and the elasticity of supply and demand.

WORKS CITED FORM: FILMSTRIP

Fashion Merchandising As Your Career. Filmstrip.
    Milady, 1980. 8 min.

PARENTHETICAL NOTE:
It would be better to name the filmstrip in your text.

The filmstrip, Fashion Merchandising As Your Career,
describes the variety of jobs available in the retail
field.

WORKS CITED FORM: FILM

The Kyocera Experiment. Film. Learning Corporation of
    America, 1981. 16 mm, 30 min.

PARENTHETICAL NOTE:
It would be better to name the film in the text of your paper.

The film, The Kyocera Experiment, shows American
employees adapting to a Japanese style of management.

5. MLA: PERFORMANCES

Begin entry with the title of performance and include information similar to that for a film. Conclude with the theater, city, and date of performance.

WORKS CITED FORM:

How to Succeed in Business Without Really Trying. By Abe
Burrows. Prods. Cy Feuer and Ernest Martin. With
Robert Morse. Forty-Sixth Street Theater, New York.
14 Oct. 1961.

PARENTHETICAL NOTE:

It would be better to mention the performance in the text of your paper.

6. MLA: WORKS OF ART

Begin with artist's name. Underline title of painting. Name the place where work is housed followed by city.

WORKS CITED FORM:

Cole, Thomas. The Architect's Dream. Toledo Museum of
Art, Toledo.

PARENTHETICAL NOTE:

It would be better to mention the work of art in the text of your paper.

7. MLA: INTERVIEWS: TELEPHONE, PERSONAL, PUBLISHED

When citing a telephone interview or a personal interview, give the name of the person being interviewed, the type of interview (telephone or personal) and the date of the interview. For a published interview give the name of person being interviewed, the identifying label *interview*, the source, the date, and the page(s).

WORKS CITED FORM: TELEPHONE

Trump, Donald. Telephone Interview. 2 Jan. 1990.

PARENTHETICAL NOTE:

Include the telephone interview in the text of your paper.

"In a recent telephone interview, Donald Trump
reported that..."

WORKS CITED FORM: PERSONAL INTERVIEW

Sims, Naomi. Personal Interview. 28 July 1991.

PARENTHETICAL NOTE:

Include the personal interview in the text of your paper.

"Naomi Sims believes that..."

WORKS CITED FORM: PUBLISHED INTERVIEW

Nakasone, Yasuhiro. Interview. By Alan M. Webber.
"Yasuhiro: The Statesman as CEO." Harvard Business
Review Mar.-Apr. 1989: 84-94.

PARENTHETICAL NOTE:

(Nakasone 84)

8. MLA: MAPS AND CHARTS

Treat map or chart like an anonymous book. Add identifying label
Map or *Chart*.

WORKS CITED FORM:

Maps of the Worlds Nations: Africa. Map. Washington:
GPO, 1977.

PARENTHETICAL NOTE:

(Maps 12)

WORKS CITED FORM:

Microsoft Software Product Line. Chart. Redmond, WA:
Microsoft, 1986.

PARENTHETICAL NOTE:
Describe the chart in the body of your paper.

9. MLA: CARTOONS AND ADVERTISEMENTS

To cite a cartoon or advertisement, give the artist's name, the title
of cartoon or advertisement (if there is any) enclosed in quotation
marks,and the identifying label *cartoon* or *advertisement*. End entry
with usual publication information.

WORKS CITED FORM:

Canon. "Born to Run." Advertisement. U.S. News & World
Report 23 Jan. 1989: 29.

PARENTHETICAL NOTE:
It is better to cite the advertisement in the text of your paper.

WORKS CITED FORM:

Vischio, Amy. Cartoon. International Business. June
1989: 11.

PARENTHETICAL NOTE:
It is better to cite the cartoon in the text of your paper.

10. MLA: LECTURES AND ADDRESSES

Give the speaker's name, the title of the speech (if known) in quotation marks, the location, and the date. If there is no title, give an appropriate identifying label (*Lecture, Address, Speech*).

WORKS CITED FORM:

Thompson, Robert T.   Class Lecture, Economics.   Eastern
        Community College.   14 Sept. 1991.

PARENTHETICAL NOTE:

Describe the lecture in the text of your paper rather than in a parenthetical note.

        Professor Robert T. Thompson explained the cyclical
nature of the American economic system.

WORKS CITED FORM:

Kirkpatrick, Jeane J.   "Remarks by the Honorable Jeane J.
        Kirkpatrick."   Opening General Sess.   NBEA
        Convention.   Chicago, 22 Mar. 1989.

PARENTHETICAL NOTE:

Include the information from a lecture in the body of your paper and avoid a parenthetical note.

        In her address, Jeane J. Kirkpatrick discussed the
future of business education in America.

11. MLA: LEGAL REFERENCE

The example is a reference to a case appealed to the U.S. Supreme Court.

WORKS CITED FORM:

Federal Trade Commission v. The Borden Co.   86 Super.
        Ct.   1966.

12. MLA: A LETTER, PUBLISHED OR UNPUBLISHED

Treat a published letter like a work in a collection. Add the date of the letter and the number if the editor has indicated one.

WORKS CITED FORM:

Ricardo, David.   "To the Editor of The Morning Chronicle
        (London)" 23 Nov 1809.   Letter III in <u>Three Letters
        on the Price of Gold</u>.   Ed. Jacob H. Holander.
        Baltimore: John Hopkins, 1903.

PARENTHETICAL NOTE:

(Ricardo 12)

To cite an unpublished letter, include the writer's name, the person to whom the letter is written, and the date.

WORKS CITED FORM:

Rothchild, Meredith.   Letter to the researcher.   17 Aug.
    1991.

PARENTHETICAL NOTE:
The letter would be described and dated in the text of your paper.

9.1.3 The Footnote/Endnote Style

Until 1984 the *MLA Handbook* recommended footnotes or endnotes instead of in-text parenthetical citations. Although the 1988 *MLA Handbook* prefers the shortened in-text citations, your instructor may ask you to use either footnotes or endnotes.

Notes give complete publishing information, either at the bottom of the page (footnotes) or at the end of the research paper (endnotes). An elevated note numeral in the text of the paper indicates that a paraphrase, summary, or quotation has been borrowed from a source. Notes are placed after the information cited and are numbered consecutively throughout the paper. To locate the publishing information for a given source, the reader finds the note with the corresponding number.

TEXT (bottom of page)

Vision and natural language for databases have been cited as the products of artificial intelligence research.[1] For example, according to Chait, artificial intelligence will allow noncomputer experts to communicate with their computers using everyday language.[2]

[1]Paul Kinnucan, "Software Tools Speed Expert System Development, "High Technology Mar. 1985: 16-20.
[2]Lawrence G. Chait, "Direct Marketing in the Epoch of Artificial Intelligence," Direct Marketing June 1985: 54.

The first time you cite a source in your paper, include all publication information for that work. Compare the following sample notes with the works-cited entries in this chapter.

Notes

[1] Donna J. Fantetti, <u>Career Directions: Special Edition</u> (Providence: P.A.R, 1987) 86.

[2] Sarah Hardesty and Nehema Jacobs, <u>The Crisis of Women in Corporate America</u> (New York: Franklin Watts, 1986) 67-77.

[3] Peter F. Drucker, <u>The Changing World of the Executive</u> (New York: Times, 1982) 22-23.

[4] Business Research Services, Inc. <u>National Directory of Minority-owned Firms</u> (Lombard, IL: BRS, 1986) 56.

[5] <u>Woman Helping Women: A State-by-State Directory of Services</u> (New York: Women's Action Alliance, 1981) 49.

[6] Geoffry Goodwin and James Mayall, eds., <u>A New International Commodity Regime</u> (New York: St. Martin's, 1980) 27-45.

[7] Caroline A. Cooper, "Careers in the Hospitality Industry," <u>Introduction to Hotel and Restaurant Management</u>, ed. Robert A. Brymer. 5th ed. (Dubuque: Kendall-Hunt, 1988) 26-34.

[8] Fred I. Greenstein and Nelson W. Polsby, eds., <u>Political Science: Scope and Theory</u>, 8 vols. (Reading, MA: Addison, 1975) 4: 37-48.

[9] Stephen P. Shao, <u>Mathematics for Management and Finance</u>, 6th ed. (Cincinnati: South-Western, 1991) 22.

[10] Anne Gibson and Timothy Fast, "Employment," <u>The Women's Atlas of the United States</u> (New York: Facts on File, 1986) 31.

[11] Theresa M. Hanafin, "Marketer Reduces Prices 25% on Marlborough Street Condos," <u>Boston Globe</u> 4 Jan. 1990: 29+.

[12] Laura Saunders, "Freezing Out the Estate Freeze," <u>Forbes</u> 17 Oct. 1988: 80-88.

[13] David N. Burt, "Managing Product Quality Through Strategic Purchasing," <u>Sloan Management Review</u> 30.3 (1989): 39-48.

SUBSEQUENT REFERENCES TO THE SAME SOURCE

Subsequent references to a work that has already been cited in a note should be written in a shortened form. Give the author's last name and a page number so that the reader can identify your reference. The Latin abbreviations *ibid* and *op. cit.* are no longer used.

```
14
  Fantetti 92.
15
  Hardesty and Jacobs 85.
```

If you are citing more than one work by one author, give the author's last name and a shortened title.

```
16
  Drucker. Changing 89.
17
  Drucker. Management 71.
```

Note: If you use notes style of documentation, you may not need to provide a works cited because the publication information is complete within the notes themselves. If your professor asks you to include a works cited or bibliography of works consulted, follow the MLA style described in this section.

9.1.4 MLA Style

To economize on space, abbreviations are commonly used in the list of works cited. In the text of your research paper, however, limit abbreviations to the parenthetical note.

MLA Rules for Shortening Publisher's Names

1. Exclude articles, business designators (*Co., Corp., Inc.*) and descriptive labels (*Books, House, Press, Publishers*). When citing a university press, however, always include the abbreviation *P* (*Columbia UP* is distinct from *Columbia U*).
2. If the publisher is the name of a single person (*E. P. Dutton, R. R. Bowker, John Wiley*), cite the last name alone (*Dutton, Bowker, Wiley*).
3. If the publisher's name includes the names of more than a single person (*Dodd, Mead, and Co.; Funk and Wagnalls, Inc.; Harcourt Brace Jovanovich, Inc.; Harper and Row Publishers, Inc.*) cite only the first name (*Dodd, Funk, Harcourt, Harper*).
4. If the publisher's name is abbreviated with capital initial letters, and the abbreviation is familiar to your reader, use the abbreviation as the publisher's name (*GPO, MLA, UP*).

ACCEPTABLE SHORTENED FORMS OF SELECTED PUBLISHERS' NAMES

ABRAMS	Harry N. Abrams, Inc.
ALLYN	Allyn and Bacon, Inc.
APPLETON	Appleton-Century-Crofts
BANTAM	Bantam Books, Inc.

BEACON	Beacon Press, Inc.
CLARENDON	Clarendon Press
CORNELL UP	Cornell University Press
DOUBLEDAY	Doubleday and Co., Inc.
FARRAR	Farrar, Straus, and Giroux, Inc.
FREE	The Free Press
GPO	Government Printing Office
HARVARD UP	Havard University Press
HEATH	D.C. Heath and Co.
HMSO	Her (His) Majesty's Stationery Office
HOLT	Holt, Rinehart, and Winston, Inc.
HOUGHTON	Houghton Mifflin Co.
KNOPF	Alfred A. Knopf, Inc.
MACMILLAN	Macmillan Publishing Co., Inc.
McGRAW	McGraw-Hill, Inc.
NORTON	W. W. Norton and Co., Inc.
PENGUIN	Penguin Books, Inc.
PRENTICE	Prentice-Hall, Inc.
RAND	Rand McNally and Co.
St. MARTIN'S	St. Martin's Press, Inc.
SCRIBNER'S	Charles Scribner's Sons
SOUTH-WESTERN	South-Western Publishing Co.
UMI	University Microfilms International
YALE UP	Yale University Press

MLA ABBREVIATIONS FOR WORDS DESIGNATING TIME

Spell out in full names of months in the text of your research paper, but abbreviate them in the list of works cited, except May, June, and July. Words denoting units of time are also spelled out in the text (*seconds, minutes, weeks, months, years, centuries*); however, some time designations are used only in abbreviated form (*A.M., P.M., AD, BC, BCE, CE*).

AD	*Anno Domini* "in the year of the Lord" (used before numerals: AD 14)
A.M.	*Ante meridiem* "before noon"
APR.	April
AUG.	August
BC	Before Christ (used after numerals: 19 BC)
BCE	Before the Common Era
CE	Common Era
CENT., CENTS.	Century, centuries
DEC.	December
FEB.	February
FRI.	Friday
HR., HRS.	Hour, hours
JAN.	January

MAR.	March
NOV.	November
OCT.	October
SAT.	Saturday
SEC., SECS.	Second, seconds
SEP., SEPT.	September
SUN.	Sunday
THURS.	Thursday
TUES.	Tuesday
WED.	Wednesday
WK., WKS.	Week, weeks
YR., YRS.,	Year, years

OTHER ABBREVIATIONS RECOMMENDED BY MLA

ABBR.	Abbreviation, abbreviated
ABR.	Abridged, abridgment
APP.	Appendix
ART.	Article
ASSN.	Association
BIBLIOG.	Bibliograph, bibliographer, bibliographic
BIOG.	Biography, biographer, biographical
BULL.	Bulletin
COL.	Column
COMP.	Compiled by, compiler
CONG.	Congress
DA	Doctor of Arts
DA, DAI	Dissertation Abstracts, Dissertation Abstracts International
DEPT.	Department
DISS.	Dissertation
DIV.	Division
DOC.	Document
ED.	Edited by, editor, edition
EDS.	Editors, editions
ENL.	Enlarged (as in "rev. and enl. ed")
ET AL.	*et alii, et aliane* "and others"
ETC.	*et cetera* "and so forth" (like most abbreviations, not appropriate in text)
FIG.	Figure
FWD.	Foreword, foreword by
ILLUS.	Illustrated by, illustrator, illustration
INTROD.	(Author of) introduction, introduced by, introduction.
KB	Kilobytes
LC	Library of Congress
LTD.	Limited

N, NN	Note, notes (used immediately after page number: 56n, 56n3, 56nn3–)
N.D.	No date (of publication)
NO.	Number (cf. number)
N.P.	No place (of publication); no publisher
N. PAG.	No pagination
NS	New series
P., PP	Page, pages (omitted before page numbers unless necessary for clarity)
PREF.	Preface, preface by
PROC.	Proceedings
PS	Postscript
PUB. (publ.)	Published by, publisher, publication
QTD.	Quoted
REV.	Revised by, revision; review, reviewed by (spell out *review* where *rev.* might be ambiguous)
RPT.	Reprinted by, reprint
SER.	Series
SESS.	Session
SUPP.	Supplement
TRANS. (tr.)	Translated by, translator, translation; transitive
TS., TSS.	Typescript, typescripts (cf. ms)
VOL., VOLS.	Volume, volumes
VS. (V)	Versus "against" (*v.* preferred in titles of legal cases)

9.2. APA DOCUMENTATION

Many college courses in business, education, and the social sciences follow the American Psychological Association (APA) style of documentation, the author-date system. The following section presents examples of the most common sources you will need to use in writing a business research paper. However, should you need to use a reference that is not provided in this section, choose the example that is most like your source and follow that format. When in doubt always cite more information than less. If you should need a more extensive discussion of the APA style, consult the *Publication Manual of the American Psychological Association*, third edition, APA, 1988.

The two basic steps of APA documentation are:

A. Preparing the parenthetical note within the body of the paper, citing the source of material by giving the author's name and the date of publication between parentheses. Use a comma to separate author's name and date. Use an ampersand (&) to join names of multiple authors.

(Freeman, Frederickson, & Miller, 1986)

(Graziano, 1987)

(Porter, 1985)

B. Preparing the "References" list, an alphabetical listing at the end, of all sources used in the paper.

References

Freeman, C., Frederickson, E., & Miller J.(1986). <u>Support staff procedures in the electronic office</u>. Englewood
   Cliffs NJ: Prentice Hall.

Graziano, L. (1987). <u>Interpreting the money supply: Human
   and institutional factors</u>. New York: Quorum.

Porter, S. (1985). <u>Love and money</u>. New York: Morrow.

9.2.1 PREPARING THE PARENTHETICAL NOTE

APA recommends a concise, clear, and accurate system for citing an extensive variety of sources. The following are models of the typical APA parenthetical citation. The source is then given as it would appear in a references list.

1. Cite the author's last name and the date of publication between parentheses.

   One researcher observes that team work involves cooperative employees who will strive for a common work
goal (Waterman, 1987).

   Place the note at the end of your sentence, before the final mark of punctuation. Notice that there is a comma between the author's name and the date of publication. Type a single space to separate name and date.

2. Use the author's name in your sentence, and provide only the date in parentheses.

   According to Waterman (1987) teamwork involves cooperative employees who will strive for a common goal.

References

Waterman, R. (1987). <u>The renewal factor: How the best get
   and keep the competitive edge</u>. Toronto: Bantam
   Books.

3. For a direct quotation use the last name of the author and the date in your sentence and place page numbers at the end of the quotation. Use p. or pp. before page number.

In a discussion on the causes of organizational change, Bridges (1988) said, "This leads to a speculator mentality among organizational leaders and fuels today's brisk market in merger and acquisitions" (p. 12).

Or for a direct quotation do not use last name of author in your sentence. Instead place last name of author, date, and page number in parentheses at the end of the quotation.

"This leads to a speculator mentality among organizational leaders and fuels today's brisk market in merger and acquisitions" (Bridges, 1988, p. 12).

References

Bridges, W. (1988). <u>Surviving corporate transition: Rational management in a world of mergers, layoffs, start-ups, takeovers, divestitures, deregulations, and new technologies</u>. New York: Doubleday.

4. Place the parenthetical note after the end punctuation if the cited passage is a lengthy direct quotation. (For quotations more than forty words long, indent five spaces from the left margin, double-spaced and without quotation marks.)

Effective listening is the key to successful leadership as one manager explains:

> There's an important emotional component to this. There's listening, and then there's engaged listening. The note-taking habit is a tip-off to the latter, but there's more to it than that. Engaged listening may be the principal mark of concern that one human being can evince for another in any setting. (Peters, 1987, p. 437)

References

Peters, T. (1987). <u>Thriving on chaos: Handbook for a management revolution</u>. New York: Knopf.

5. To cite sources within a single sentence, place each note after the statements each supports.

Waterman (1987) asserts the importance of visible management attention to motivate employees (p. 11), and Peters (1987) adds effective management as a component of visible management (p. 435).

6. Do not repeat the author's name in second or subsequent references to the sources, unless a different reference intervenes.

L. G. Chait (1985) examines some computer systems capable of performing intelligent human activities that involve language, learning, and problem solving (p. 54). Some of the most recent developments in this area are already a marketplace reality. Artificial intelligence, he believes, will expand our capabilities in all fields of human endeavor (p. 56). Even the areas of machine vision and natural language for databases have been cited as the products of artificial intelligence research (Kinnucan, 1985 p. 17). For example, according to Chait (1985) artificial intelligence will allow noncomputer experts to communicate with their computers using everyday language (p. 54).

References

Chait, L. (1985, June). Direct marketing in the epoch of artificial intelligence. <u>Direct Marketing</u>, pp. 54-61.
Kinnucan, P. (1985, March). Software tools speed expert system development. <u>High Technology</u>, pp. 16-20.

7. If you use more than one work by a single author, use the author's name and the date in your sentence, and add a shortened version of the title of the book to each note, followed by the page number(s). Underline the shortened title. Because each reference below is a direct quotation, add the page number preceded by p. or pp. to the parenthetical note.

To A. Cox (1988), an experienced executive recruiter, "warmth is the appetite for showing and being shown acceptance" (Making of Achiever, p. 9). At the corporate level an atmosphere of warmth promotes a feeling of acceptance. Cox asserts that "the inter-personal network" must be as solid as the ties that bind a family, neighborhood, or religious institute (Achiever's Profile, p. 68).

References

Cox, A. (1985). The making of the achiever: How to win distinction in your company. New York: Dodd, Mead.

Cox, A. (1988). The achiever's profile: One hundred questions and answers to sharpen your executive instincts. New York: Amacon.

8. When citing a work with no author, list a shortened version of the title followed by the date of publication. Begin the shortened title with the first word of the full title (excluding *A, An, The*) so that the correct references citation can be found. For example, an unsigned magazine article entitled "Public Service Ads Top $1 Billion in '87," might be shortened to *"Public Service."* Capitalize all significant words of the shortened title of the article. Put quotation marks around shortened title.

("Public Service", 1988)

References

Public service ads top $1 billion in '87. (1988, June 6), Advertising Age, p. 72.

9. When citing a work with two authors, always cite both names every time the reference occurs in text.

Doerflinger and Rivkin (1987) agree that the era of computers, telecommunications, biotechnology, and space technologies are evidence of another Industrial Revolution.

When citing a work with three, four, or five authors, cite all authors the first time the reference occurs; in subsequent citations include only the last name of the first author followed by *et al.* (the Latin expression for "and others."), and the year.

FIRST CITATION:

Following the Civil War period, the Industrial Revolution expanded the need for farming and textile products in America (Sandage, Fryburger, & Rotzoll, 1989).

SUBSEQUENT CITATION:

(Sandage et al., 1989).

When citing a work by six or more authors, cite the last name of the first author followed by *et al.*, and the date in the first reference and in subsequent references. In the reference list, however, spell out names of all authors.

Aaron et al. (1986) stress the possibility that welfare payments may, in the long run, "perpetuate poverty, especially among female-headed families in inner cities" (pp. 74-75).

References

Aaron, H. J., Galper, H., Pechman, J.A., Perry, G.L., Rivlin, A.M., & Schultze, C.(1986). Economic choices: 1987. Washington, DC: Brookings Institute.

Doerflinger, T., & Rivkin J.L. (1987). Risks and reward: Venture capital and the making of America's great industries. New York: Random House.

Sandage, C.H., Fryburger, V., & Rotzoll K. (1989) Advertising: Theory and practice. New York: Longman.

10. To cite a work by a corporate author, integrate the information with your sentence. For clarity it would be better to name the corporate author and the date of publication in your sentence.

American Telephone and Telegraph's Annual Report for 1988 announced a new European mobile phone system to meet motorists' needs.

Note: When the publisher is the same as the author, write *author* in publisher's position.

Reference

American Telephone and Telegraph. (1988). <u>Annual Report</u>.
   Author.

11. To cite one volume from a multivolume work, indicate in the
    parenthetical reference the editor's name and date of publication.

   John Maynard Keynes asserts that theater and arts
exist for public and not for private purposes (Moggridge,
1982).

References

Moggridge, D. (Ed.) (1982). <u>The collected writings of</u>
   <u>John Maynard Keynes</u>. (Vols. 1-30). London: Macmillan.

12. To cite more than one work in a single parenthetical reference,
    cite each work as you normally would in a reference, but use
    semicolons to separate the citations.

(Shamoon, 1984; Sahgal and Crawford, 1985)

(Lowry et al., 1990; Crosby, 1986)

References

Crosby, P. B. (1986). <u>Running things: The art of making</u>
   <u>things happen</u>. New York: McGraw-Hill.

Lowry, J.R., Weinrich, B.W., Steade, R. D. (1990).
   <u>Business in today's world</u>. Cincinnati, OH:
   South-Western.

Sahgal, P., & Crawford, D. (1985, March). The new moguls
   of computerized investing. <u>Wall Street Computer</u>
   <u>Review</u>, pp. 35-48.

Shamoon, S. (1984, December). The bank is a true believer
   in slick slides and charts. <u>Management Technology</u>,
   pp. 42-54.

9.2.2 PREPARING THE REFERENCES LIST

   In writing your research paper you will borrow material from a variety of books, periodicals, journals, and nonprint sources. To avoid
plagiarism you are obligated to indicate where you found the borrowed

facts, opinions, or quotations. The APA style of documentation recommends that you acknowledge your sources by keying references in the text to a references list at the end of your research paper. The references list simplifies documentation because it includes all of the wide variety of sources used in your paper.

Follow these general APA guidelines to prepare the list of references.

1. Begin the references list on its own page following the body of the research paper. If the conclusion of your paper appears on page 10, the references list appears on page 11.

2. Begin the first line of each entry flush with the left margin, and indent the subsequent line or lines three spaces from the left margin. Double space between successive lines of an entry and between entries.

Lu, D. (1987). <u>Inside corporate Japan: The art of fumble-free management</u>. Cambridge: Productivity Press.

Ming, Z. (1989, July 24). Beijing continues to open the door. <u>Beijing Review</u>, pp. 19-20.

Quinn, J. B. (1979). <u>Everyone's money book</u>. New York: Delacourt.

3. Alphabetize entries according to author's last name. Reverse names of all authors and use initials for the first and middle names of all authors. When there are two or more authors, use an ampersand (&) before the name of the last author.

Gasteneau, G. L.

Stigum, M.

Tewles, R.J., & Brady, E.S.

McCracken, P., Weidenbaum, M.L., Ritter, L.S., & Kavesh, R.A.

4. To list more than one work by the same author, give the name in the first reference and all subsequent references. Arrange the references by the year of publication, the earliest first.

Friedman, M. (1968). <u>Dollars and deficits: Living with America's economic problems</u>. Englewood Cliffs, NJ: Prentice Hall.

Friedman, M. (1969). <u>The optimum quantity of money and other essays</u>. Chicago: Aldine.

Friedman, M. (1973). <u>Money and economic development</u>. New York: Praeger.

Friedman, M. (1975). <u>There's no such thing as a free lunch</u>. La Salle, IL: Open Court.

5. To identify works by the same author(s) with the same date of publication, add the suffix *a, b, c,* and so forth to the date: (1991a, 1991b, 1991c).

Osigweh, C.A.B. (1985a, May-June). Puzzles or problems? Cutting through the manager's dilemma. <u>Business Horizons</u>, pp. 69-74.

Osigweh, C.A.B. (1985b). <u>Professional management: An evolutionary perspective</u>. Dubuque, IA: Kendall/Hunt.

6. To ensure completeness type a continuous line under the entire title of a book. Use uppercase and lowercase letters. Capitalize only the first word of the title of the book and the first word of the subtitle after the colon. Capitalize any proper nouns in the title. Place a period at the end of the title. Do not underline the period.

<u>Start up telemarketing: How to launch a profitable sales operation</u>.
<u>Unnecessary choices: The hidden life of the executive woman</u>.
<u>Tax planning for acquisitions in the United States</u>.

7. Underline the titles of journals, magazines, and newspapers. Capitalize the first word and all significant words in the title. Use lowercase letters for articles and short prepositions. Do not drop the article *The* from the name of a periodical. Cite the name as it appears on the masthead of the newspaper.

<u>IBM Journal of Research</u>
<u>Telemarketing: The Magazine of Business Telecommunications</u>
<u>U.S. News & World Report</u>
<u>The Boston Globe</u>
<u>USA Today</u>
<u>Chicago Tribune</u>
<u>The Christian Science Monitor</u>

8. Capitalize only the first word of the title and subtitle of an article. Capitalize any proper nouns. Do not underline the title of the article. Do not enclose the title of the article in quotation marks. End the title of the article with a period.

Consumers in 1988: The year in review.

Family carries on booming business.

The next generation.

The handicapped make headway on Madison Avenue.

9. Underline a title of a book when it occurs within a title of an article.

Comer: Nation of strangers hinders education.

10. When citing a shorter work that appears in a larger work, indicate that the shorter work is in a larger work: *in C.D. Schewe (Ed.)*. When the editor's name is not in the author position, do not invert the name; use initials and last name.

Neugarten, B. (1985). Acting one's age: New rules for old. In C.D.Schewe (Ed.), The elderly market: selected readings. Chicago: American Marketing Association.

11. Place a period followed by one space after author and date.

Suzaki, K. (1987). The new manufacturing challenge: Techniques for continuous improvement.

Jennings, D. (1989). Self-Made women: Twelve of America's leading entrepreneurs talk about success, self-image, and the superwoman.

12. When citing a journal article do not use *vol.* before the numbers. Underline the Arabic number followed by inclusive page numbers. Do not use *pp.* in reference to journal articles. Use a comma between volume number and pages. End citation with a period.

Note: Express all page numbers in full.

Gersick, C.J.G. (1989). Marking time: Predictable transitions in task groups. Academy of Management Journal, 32, 274-309.

13. When citing a magazine or newspaper article use *pp.* before page numbers.

Moore, T. (1989, January 23). The bust of '89. US News & World Report, pp. 36-43.

14. If an article appears on discontinuous pages, give all page numbers and separate the numbers with a comma. Write out the months of the year in full.

How cosmetic makers are touching up their strategies. (1985, September 23). Business Week, pp. 66, 68, 73.

APA GUIDE: CITING BOOKS

The numbered list that follows will help you locate the type of source you will need to cite your reference. On the pages that follow you will find examples of references and parenthetical notes for each type of source on the list.

APA DOCUMENTATION
CITING BOOKS: ARRANGEMENT OF REQUIRED INFORMATION

An entry in a list of works cited has three main divisions: (1) author's name followed by date of publication, a period and one space, (2) title of book followed by period and one space, (3) place of publication followed by colon, one space, and publisher.

```
Biggart, N. W. (1989). Charismatic capitalism: Direct
    selling organizations in America. Chicago: University
    of Chicago Press.
```

1. Author's name and date of publication: Biggart, N. W. (1989).
2. Title of book: Charismatic capitalism: Direct selling organizations in America.
3. Place of publication: Chicago:
4. Name of publisher: University of Chicago Press.

1. APA: BOOK BY ONE AUTHOR
REFERENCE:

Fantetti, D. J. (1987). Career directions: Special
edition. Providence: P.A.R.

PARENTHETICAL NOTE:

(Fantetti, 1987)

2. APA: BOOK BY TWO, THREE, FOUR, OR, FIVE AUTHORS
Invert all authors' names; give last names and initials for all authors. Use commas to separate authors. With two or more authors use an ampersand (&) before the last author.

REFERENCE:

Hardesty, S. & Jacobs, N. (1986). The crisis of women in
corporate America. New York: Franklin Watts.

PARENTHETICAL NOTE:

(Hardesty & Jacobs, 1986)

REFERENCE:

Urban, G. L., Hauser, J. R., & Dholakia N. (1987).
Essentials of new product management. Englewood
Cliffs, NJ: Prentice Hall.

Note: If the city is unfamiliar, add the state for clarity.

PARENTHETICAL NOTE: FIRST REFERENCE

(Urban, Hauser, & Dholakia, 1987)

SUBSEQUENT REFERENCE

(Urban et al., 1987)

3. APA: BOOK BY SIX OR MORE AUTHORS
The last names in references with six or more authors are spelled out. In the parenthetical note cite only the last name of the first author followed by *et al.*
REFERENCE:

Aaron, H. J., Galper, H., Pechman, J. A., Perry, G. L.,
Rivlin, A. M., & Schultze, C. (1986). Economic
Choices: 1987. Washington: Brookings Institute.

PARENTHETICAL NOTE:

(Aaron et al., 1986)

4. APA: BOOK BY TWO AUTHORS WITH SAME LAST NAME
REFERENCE:

Lott, C. S., & Lott, O. C. (1985). How to land a better
  job. Lincolnwood, IL: VGM Career Horizons.

PARENTHETICAL NOTE:

(Lott & Lott, 1985)

5. APA: TWO OR MORE BOOKS BY SAME AUTHOR
REFERENCE:

Drucker, P. F. (1964). Managing for results. New York:
  Harper and Row.
Drucker, P. F. (1974). Management: Tasks,
  responsibilities, practices. New York: Harper and
  Row.
Drucker, P. F. (1982). The changing world of the
  executive. New York: Times.

PARENTHETICAL NOTE:

(Drucker, 1982)

6. APA: BOOK WITH COLLABORATOR
Begin the entry with the author's name followed by a comma. Add
with and the name of the collaborator.
REFERENCE:

Cunningham, M., with Fran Schumer (1984). Powerplay:
  What really happened at Bendix. New York:
  Linden-Simon.

PARENTHETICAL NOTE:

(Cunningham, 1984)

7. APA: BOOK BY A CORPORATE AUTHOR
A corporate author may be a group whose individual members are
not identified on the title page. Place the corporate author in the position of the author. When author and publisher are the same, write
author in the position of the publisher.
REFERENCE:

Business Research Services, Inc. (1986). National
  directory of minority-owned firms. Lombard, IL:
  Author.

PARENTHETICAL NOTE:

(Business Research, 1986)

8. APA: BOOK BY ANONYMOUS AUTHOR
If the book has no author's name on the title page, begin the entry with the title of the book.
REFERENCE:

Women helping women: A state-by-state directory of
    services (1981). New York: Women's Action Alliance.

PARENTHETICAL NOTE:

(Women Helping Women, 1981)

9. APA: BOOK WITH EDITOR OR COMPILER
Begin the entry with the name of the editor or editors. Put *Ed.* or *Eds.* in parentheses [*Eds.*].
REFERENCE:

Goodwin, G., & Mayall, J. (Eds.). (1980). A new
    international commodity regime. New York: St.
    Martin's Press.

PARENTHETICAL NOTE:

(Goodwin & Mayall, 1980)

REFERENCE:

Andriole, S. J. (Ed.). (1985). Corporate crisis
    management. Princeton, NJ: Petrocelli.

PARENTHETICAL NOTE:

(Andriole, 1985)

10. APA: BOOK WITH AUTHOR AND EDITOR
Write the author's name and the title of book. After the title write the name of the editor.
REFERENCE:

Galbraith, J. K. (1971). Economics and laughter. A. D.
    Williams (Ed.). Boston: Houghton Mifflin.

PARENTHETICAL NOTE:

(Galbraith, 1971)

11. APA: PUBLISHER'S IMPRINT

An imprint identifies the many groups of books of a publisher. When you cite a book under an imprint, give the name of the imprint followed by a hyphen and the name of the publisher: *Anchor-Doubleday, Camelot-Avon, and Linden-Simon.*

REFERENCE:

Gardenswartz, L. & Rowe A. (1987). <u>What it takes: Good news from 100 of America's top professional and business women</u>. New York: Dolphin-Doubleday.

PARENTHETICAL NOTE:

(Gardenswartz & Rowe, 1987)

12. APA: ANTHOLOGY OR COMPILATION

Begin with the name of the editor or compiler followed by *(Ed)*.

REFERENCE:

Brymer, R. A. (Ed.). (1988). <u>Introduction to hotel and restaurant management</u> (5th ed.) Dubuque, IA: Kendall-Hunt.

PARENTHETICAL NOTE:

(Brymer, 1988)

13. APA: WORK IN AN ANTHOLOGY

At the beginning of the entry state the author's name and title of the article you are citing. When an editor's name is not in the author position, do not invert the name; use initials and last name.

REFERENCE:

Cooper, C. A. (1988). Careers in the hospitality industry. In R. A. Brymer (Ed.), <u>Introduction to hotel and restaurant management</u> (5th ed.) (pp. 26-34). Dubuque, IA: Kendall-Hunt.

PARENTHETICAL NOTE:

(Cooper, 1988)14.

14. APA: INTRODUCTION, PREFACE, FOREWORD, AFTERWORD

To cite information from an introduction, a preface, a foreword, or an afterword, begin with the name of its author, then identify the part being cited. Capitalize the identified part. If the writer of the "part" is also the author of the complete work, use only the last name after *By*. If the writer of the part is different from the author of the complete work, cite the author of the work after the title. Give the full name, in normal order, preceded by the word *By*.

REFERENCE:

Nivens, B. (1982). Introduction. The black woman's career
   guide. By Nivens. New York: Anchor-Doubleday.
   pp.xii-xiv.

PARENTHETICAL NOTE:

(Nivens, 1982)

REFERENCE:

Blanchard, K. (1988). Foreword. Swim with the sharks
   without being eaten alive: Outsell, outmanage, and
   outnegotiate your competition. By Harvey Mackey. New
   York: Morrow. pp. 7-10.

PARENTHETICAL NOTE:

(Blanchard, 1988)

REFERENCE:

Hamlin, S. (1988). Afterword. How to talk so people
   listen: The real key to job success. By Hamlin. New
   York: Harper and Row. pp. 257-258.

PARENTHETICAL NOTE:

(Hamlin 257-258)

15. APA MULTIVOLUME WORK

When you have used two or more volumes of a multivolume work, give the total number of volumes (*Vols. 1-8*) in the work. Place this information between the title and the publication information.

REFERENCE:

Greenstein, F. I., & Polsby, N. W. (Eds.). (1975).
   Political science: Scope and theory. (Vols.
   1-8).Reading, MA: Addison Wesley.

PARENTHETICAL NOTE:

(Greenstein & Polsby, 1975)

16. APA: EDITION OTHER THAN THE FIRST

The title page will indicate the edition of the book. A book that gives no edition number on its title page is probably a first edition. You need not indicate a first edition in your bibliography. If, however, you are using an edition other than the first edition, identify it in your entry as follows: (2nd ed., 3rd ed., 4th ed.). When more than one copyright date is listed, cite the latest date.

REFERENCE:

Shao, S.P. (1991). Mathematics for management and
    finance. (6th ed.) Cincinnati: South-Western.

PARENTHETICAL NOTE:

(Shao, 1991)

17. APA: BOOK IN A SERIES

If the book you are citing is part of a series, include the series name, neither underlined nor enclosed in quotation marks. Include the series number followed by a period before the publication information.

REFERENCE:

Knight, J. B., & Salter C. A. (1987). Food service
    standards in resorts. L.J. Minor Foodservice
    Standards Ser. 6. New York: CBI-Van Nostrand.

PARENTHETICAL NOTE:

(Knight & Salter, 1987)

18. APA: REPUBLISHED BOOK

The original place of publication, publisher, and date of publication may precede the current publication information.

REFERENCE:

Presnell, L.S., (Ed.). (1975) Money and banking in Japan
    (S. Nishimura, Trans.). London: MacMillan. (Original
    work published Japan: Bank of Japan, 1969)

PARENTHETICAL NOTE:

(Presnell, 1969/1975)

19. APA: PUBLISHED PROCEEDINGS OF A CONFERENCE
REFERENCE:

Zanot, E. (1981). Public attitude toward advertising. In
    H. K. Hunt (Ed.), Advertising in a new age (pp.

142-146). Proceedings of the annual conference of the American Academy of Advertising. Provo, UT: American Academy of Advertising.

PARENTHETICAL NOTE

(Zanot, 1981)

20. APA: TRANSLATION

Give the author's name first. If there is an editor and a translator give both names with abbreviated titles *Trans.* or *Ed.*

REFERENCE:

Montagne, P. (1977). The new Larousse gastronomique. (C. Turgeon, Ed.). (M. Hunter, Trans.). New York: Crown.

PARENTHETICAL NOTE:

(Montagne, 1977)

21. APA: BOOK PUBLISHED BEFORE 1900

You may omit the name of the publisher. Use a comma instead of a colon after the place of publication.

REFERENCE:

McVickar, J. (1825). Outlines of political economy. New York.

PARENTHETICAL NOTE:

(McVickar, 1825)

22. APA: A PAMPHLET

Cite a pamphlet as you would a book.

REFERENCE:

Labor market review. (1988). Richmond: Virginia Employment Commission.

PARENTHETICAL NOTE:
Capitalize and underline the words of the title.

(Labor Market Review, 1988)

23. APA: GOVERNMENT PUBLICATION

REFERENCE:

United States: Office of Consumer Affairs. (1988) Consumer's resource handbook (4th ed.) Washington, DC: Government Printing Office.

PARENTHETICAL NOTE:
To avoid a lengthy note, name the document in the body of the paper.

"This information is based on material from...."

24. APA: ARTICLE IN A REFERENCE WORK
REFERENCE:

Gibson, A., & Fast T. (1986). <u>Employment: The women's atlas of the United States</u>. New York: Facts on File.

PARENTHETICAL NOTE:

(Gibson & Fast, 1986)

25. APA: BOOK IN A LANGUAGE OTHER THAN ENGLISH
REFERENCE:

Odaka, K. (1984). <u>Nihonteki keiei: Shinwa to Genjitsu</u> <Japanese management: A forward looking analysis>. Tokyo: Chuo Koron-sha.

PARENTHETICAL NOTE:

(Odaka, 1984)

APA GUIDE: CITING NEWSPAPERS, MAGAZINES AND PERIODICALS

1. Article from newspaper, author named, p. 177
2. Article from newsapaper, no author named, pp. 177–178
3. Article from newspaper, different editions, p. 178
4. Article from newspaper, editorial, p. 178
5. Article from weekly or biweekly magazine, p. 178
6. Article from monthly or bimonthly magazine, pp. 178–179
7. Unsigned article from magazine, p. 179
8. Article in a scholarly journal with continuous pagination, p. 179
9. Article in a scholarly journal that pages each issue separately, pp. 179–180
10. Letter to the editor, p. 180
11. A review, p. 180.
12. An abstract from *Dissertation Abstracts* or *Dissertation Abstracts International*, p. 180

CITING PERIODICALS: ARRANGEMENT OF REQUIRED INFORMATION
Periodicals include newspapers, magazines, and scholarly journals. An entry for an article in a periodical has four main divisions: (1) author

and date, followed by a period and one space; (2) title of article, in uppercase and lowercase letters. Do not enclose in quotation marks. (End the title with a period and one space); (3) name of periodical underlined, with first word and proper nouns capitalized; and (4) publication information. For scholarly journals the publication information includes the journal title, the volume number, and the inclusive page numbers of the article.

```
Bertrand, K. Get ready for global capitalism. (1990,
     January). Business Marketing, pp. 42-44, 49-50, 52.
```

1. Author and date: Bertrand, K. (1990, January).
2. Title of the article: Get ready for global capitalism.
3. Name of the magazine underlined: Business Marketing.
4. Page(s) of publication: pp. 42-44, 49-50, 52.

Note: When an article is not printed on consecutive pages, indicate all pages of the article.

```
Sabath, A. M. (1989, June 20). Client sees restaurant as
     an extension of your office. The Washington Times,
     sec. E, p. 9.
```

1. Author's name and date: Sabath, A. M. (1989, June 20).
2. Title of article: Client sees restaurant as an extension of your office.
3. Name of newspaper underlined: The Washington Times.
4. Section and Page number of publication: sec. E, p. 9.

1. APA: ARTICLE FROM NEWSPAPER, AUTHOR NAMED

In this example the section is numbered not lettered.

REFERENCE:

```
Hanafin, T. M. (1990, January 4). Marketer reduces prices
     25% on Marborough Street condos. The Boston Globe,
     p. 29, 33.
```

PARENTHETICAL NOTE:

```
(Hanafin, 1990)
```

2. APA: ARTICLE FROM NEWSPAPER, NO AUTHOR NAMED

Put the title of the article in the author position. Alphabetize by the first significant word in the title.

REFERENCE:

The TV commercial tries on some disguises. (1985,
    September 1). The New York Times, p. 14.

PARENTHETICAL NOTE:

("TV Commercial," 1985)

3. APA: ARTICLE FROM NEWSPAPER, DIFFERENT EDITION
REFERENCE:

Miller, M.W. (1989, July 5). A new picture for computer
    graphics: The next wave in PC's may be use of video.
    The Wall Street Journal, eastern ed., sec. B, p. 1.

PARENTHETICAL NOTE:

(Miller, 1989)

4. APA: ARTICLE FROM NEWSPAPER, EDITORIAL
REFERENCE:

Forest service's watershed blitz. (1989, December 24).
    <Editorial>. Seattle Post-Intelligencer, sec. E, P. 2.

PARENTHETICAL NOTE:

("Forest," 1989)

5. APA: ARTICLE FROM WEEKLY OR BIWEEKLY MAGAZINE
Give the exact date of publication: the year, the month written out
in full, and the day.
REFERENCE:

Saunders, L. (1988, October 17). Freezing out the estate
    freeze. Forbes, pp. 80-88.

PARENTHETICAL NOTE:

(Saunders, 1988)

6. APA: ARTICLE FROM MONTHLY OR BIMONTHLY MAGAZINE
REFERENCE:

Lodge, A. (1985, October). That is the most you will ever
    pay. Journal of Accountancy, p. 44.

PARENTHETICAL NOTE:

(Lodge, 1985)

REFERENCE:

Beadle, C. E. (1988, November-December) The future of
    employee benefits. Compensation and Benefits Review,
    pp. 35-44.

PARENTHETICAL NOTE:

(Beadle, 1988)

7. APA: UNSIGNED ARTICLE FROM MAGAZINE

Put the title of the article in the author position. Use a shortened form of the title in the parenthetical note. Capitalize short title and enclose in quotation marks.

REFERENCE:

Determining how ads are seen. (1982, February). Dun's
    Business Month pp. 85-86.

PARENTHETICAL NOTE:

("Determining How," 1982)

8. APA: ARTICLE IN A SCHOLARLY JOURNAL WITH CONTINUOUS PAGINATION

If the journal uses continuous pagination throughout the annual volume, then after the title place the volume number, underlined, and the page numbers without *p.* or *pp.* (For example, when the first issue ends on page 200, and the second issue begins on page 201.)End entry with a period.

REFERENCE:

Lien, D. D. (1989). Cash settlement provisions on futures
    contracts. Journal of Futures Markets, 9, 263-270.

PARENTHETICAL NOTE:

(Lien, 1989)

9. APA: ARTICLE IN A SCHOLARLY JOURNAL THAT PAGES EACH ISSUE SEPARATELY

Some journals begin each issue with page 1. Give the volume number, underlined; the issue number in parentheses; and page numbers without *p.* or *pp.* End the citation with a period.

REFERENCE:

Burt, D. N. (1989). Managing product quality through
strategic purchasing. <u>Sloan Management Review</u>, <u>30</u>(3),
39-40.

PARENTHETICAL NOTE:

(Burt, 1989)

10. APA: LETTER TO THE EDITOR
REFERENCE:

Heller, L. I. (1988, November). <Letter to the editor>.
<u>Business Month</u>, p. 6.

PARENTHETICAL NOTE:

(Heller, 1988)

11. APA: A REVIEW
REFERENCES:

Liles, S. (1989, June 21).<Review of Entrepreneurial
Woman>. <u>USA Today</u>, sec. B, p. 4.

PARENTHETICAL NOTE:

(Liles, 1989)

12. APA: AN ABSTRACT FROM *DISSERTATION ABSTRACTS* OR *DISSERTATION ABSTRACTS INTERNATIONAL*
REFERENCE:

Al-Loughani, N. E. (1987). The impact of business groups
on domestic lending: An investigation of the
portfolio behavior of commercial banks in Kuwait.
<u>Dissertation Abstracts International</u>, 49, 8818895.
(Golden Gate University)

PARENTHETICAL NOTE:

(Al-Loughani, 1987)

OTHER SOURCES

CITING OTHER SOURCES:

1. APA: COMPUTER SOFTWARE

Give the name of the writer of the program, if there is one. Give the title of the program, underlined; the date; the version of the program (*vers.*); and the identifying label (*computer program*); the place of publication; and the distributor. At the end of the entry, enclose in parentheses any pertinent information.

REFERENCE:

```
dBase III PLUS. (1986). Vers. 1.0. <Computer program>
    Torrance, CA: Ashton-Tate. (IBM/MS-DOS)
```

PARENTHETICAL NOTE:

It is better to name the software in the body of the paper.

2. APA: MATERIAL FROM A COMPUTER SERVICE

Treat information obtained from a computer service, such as Dialog or BRS, as other printed material. At the end of the entry cite the name of the service, and the identifying number.

REFERENCE:

```
Grensing, L. (1987, January) An AA primer: Eight tips on
    affirmative action. Management World, pp. 34-35.
    (DIALOG Information Services, file 75, No. 0362837)
```

PARENTHETICAL NOTE:

```
(Grensing, 1987)
```

3. APA: TELEVISION AND RADIO PROGRAMS

Include the title of the program, underlined, and the date of broadcast; the director, narrator, producer; the network (PBS); the local station; and the city.

RERERENCE:

Wall Street week (1990, January 5). With L. Rukeyser. (G.
    Beneman, Director). (J.H. Davis & R. Dubroff.
    Producers) PBS, WGBH, Maryland Public Television,
    Owings Mills.

PARENTHETICAL NOTE:
It is better to name the program in the text of your paper.

4. APA: AUDIO RECORDING, VIDEO CASSETTE, FILMSTRIP, FILM

Include the speaker; the date; the title, underlined; the director; the distributor; and the year. After the title specify the medium in brackets ⟨Sound Recording⟩. Add any pertinent information such as the writers and the performers.

REFERENCE: AUDIO RECORDING

Nieremberg, G. I. (Speaker). (1983). Nieremberg on
    negotiating. ⟨Sound Recording⟩. Waco, TX: Success
    Motivation.

PARENTHETICAL NOTE:
It would be better to name the recording in the text.

    In the audio recording, Nieremberg on Negotiating,
Nieremberg describes skills helpful in persuading people
to reach agreements.

REFERENCE: VIDEOTAPE

Schoumacher, D. (Speaker). (1986). Economics USA: Perfect
    Competition ⟨Videotape⟩. (L. Barbesh, Producer &
    Director). Chicago: Films, Inc.

PARENTHETICAL NOTE:
It would be better to name the videotape in the text.

    In the video cassette, Economics USA: Perfect
Competition, Schoumacher illustrates the concepts of
competition, and the elasticity of supply and demand.

REFERENCE: FILMSTRIP

Fashion merchandising as your career ⟨Filmstrip⟩. (1980).
    Bronx, NY: Milady.

PARENTHETICAL NOTE:

It would be better to name the filmstrip in your text.

> The filmstrip, <u>Fashion Merchandising As Your Career</u>, describes the variety of jobs available in the retail field.

REFERENCES: FILM

<u>The Kyocera experiment</u> <Film>. (1981) New York: Learning
    Corporation of America.

PARENTHETICAL NOTE:
It would be better to name the film in the text of your paper.

> The film, <u>The Kyocera Experiment</u>, shows American employees adapting to a Japanese style of management.

5. APA: PERFORMANCES
Begin entry with the title of performance and include information similar to that for a film. Conclude with the theater, city, and date of performance.

REFERENCE:

Feuer, C. & Martin, E.(Producers). (1961, October 14).
    <u>How to succeed in business without really trying</u>
    <Play>. By A. Burrows. With R. Morse. Forty-Second
    Street Theater, New York.

PARENTHETICAL NOTE:
It would be better to name the performance in the text of your paper.

6. APA: WORKS OF ART
Begin with artist's name. Underline title of painting. Enclose art work in parentheses. Name the place where work is housed, followed by city.

REFERENCE:

Cole, T. <u>The Architect's Dream</u> <Art work>. Toledo: Toledo
    Museum of Art.

PARENTHETICAL NOTE:
It would be better to mention the work of art in the text of your paper.

7. APA: INTERVIEWS: TELEPHONE, PERSONAL, PUBLISHED
Because telephone and personal interviews do not provide recoverable data, do not include them in the references list. Cite personal

communications in the text only. Provide initials and last name of communicator and as exact a date as possible.

PARENTHETICAL NOTE:

Include the telephone interview or personal interview in the text of your paper.

"In a recent interview, D. Trump, (personal communication, February 2, 1990) reported that..."

REFERENCE: PUBLISHED INTERVIEW

Nakasone, Y. (1989, March-April). <Interview by Alan M. Webber>. Yasuhiro: The statesman as CEO. Harvard Business Review, pp. 84-94.

PARENTHETICAL NOTE:

(Nakasone, 1989)

8. APA: MAPS AND CHARTS

Treat map or chart like an anonymous book. Add identifying label *Map* or *Chart*.

REFERENCE:

Maps of the worlds nations: Africa <Map>. (1977). Washington DC: Government Printing Office.

PARENTHETICAL NOTE:

(Map, 1977)

REFERENCE:

Microsoft software product line <Chart>. (1986). Redmond, WA: Microsoft.

PARENTHETICAL NOTE:

Describe the chart in the body of your paper.

9. APA: CARTOONS AND ADVERTISEMENTS

To cite a cartoon or advertisement, give the artist's name, the title of cartoon or advertisement (if there is any) enclosed in quotation marks, and the identifying label *cartoon* or *advertisement*. End entry with usual publication information.

REFERENCE:

Canon. (1989, January 23). Born to Run <Advertisement>. U.S. News & World Report, p. 29.

PARENTHETICAL NOTE:

It is better to cite the advertisement in the text of your paper.

REFERENCE:

Vischio, A. (1989, June). <Cartoon>. International
   Business, p. 11.

PARENTHETICAL NOTE:
It is better to cite the cartoon in the text of your paper.

10. APA: LECTURES AND ADDRESSES
Give the speaker's name, the title of the speech (if known) in quotation marks, the location, and the date. If there is no title, give an appropriate identifying label (Lecture, Address, Speech).

REFERENCE:

Thompson, R. T. (1991, September 14). <Class lecture,
   Economics>. Eastern Community College.

PARENTHETICAL NOTE:
Describe the lecture in the text of your paper rather than in a parenthetical note.

   Professor R. T. Thompson explained the cyclical
nature of the American economic system.

REFERENCE:

Kirkpatrick, J. J. (1989, March 22). Remarks by
   the Honorable Jeane J. Kirkpatrick. Lecture given at
   National Business Educators Convention, Chicago.

PARENTHETICAL NOTE:
   Include the information from a lecture in the body of your paper and avoid a parenthetical note.

   In her address, J. J. Kirkpatrick discussed the
future of business education in America.

11. APA: LEGAL REFERENCE
This example is a case appealed to the U.S. Supreme Court.

REFERENCE

Federal Trade Commission v. The Borden Co., 86 S. Ct.
   1092 (1966).

PARENTHETICAL NOTE:
It would be better to name the case in the text of your paper.

12. APA: AN UNPUBLISHED LETTER

To cite an unpublished letter, include the writer's name, the date, and the person to whom the letter is written.

REFERENCE:

```
Rothchild, M. (1991, August 17). <Letter to the
    researcher>.
```

PARENTHETICAL NOTE:

The letter would be described and dated in the text of your paper.

9.2.3 APA STYLE

1. APA accepts the following abbreviations for parts of books and other publications:

chap.	chapter
ed.	edition
re. ed.	revised edition
2nd ed.	second edition
Ed. (Eds.)	Editor (Editors)
Trans.	translator(s)
p. (pp.)	page (pages)
vol.	volume (as in Vol. 2)
vols.	volumes (as in 2 vols.)
No.	number
Pt.	part
Tech. Rep.	Technical Report

2. Arabic numerals: APA journals use Arabic numerals for all numbers in reference lists (for example, *Vol. 3*, not *Vol. III*).
3. Abbreviations for states and territories: In the references list use the official two-letter U.S. Postal Service abbreviations as listed below. In the text of the paper, however, spell out the name of the state to avoid confusion.

Alabama	AL
Alaska	AK
American Samoa	AS
Arizona	AZ

Arkansas	AR
California	CA
Canal Zone	CZ
Colorado	CO
Connecticut	CT
Delaware	DE
District of Columbia	DC
Florida	FL
Georgia	GA
Guam	GU
Hawaii	HI
Idaho	ID
Illinois	IL
Indiana	IN
Iowa	IA
Kansas	KS
Kentucky	KY
Louisiana	LA
Maine	MA
Maryland	MD
Massachusetts	MA
Michigan	MI
Minnesota	MN
Mississippi	MS
Missouri	MO
Montana	MT
Nebraska	NE
Nevada	NV
New Hampshire	NH
New Jersey	NJ
New Mexico	NM
New York	NY
North Carolina	NC
North Dakota	ND
Ohio	OH
Oklahoma	OK
Oregon	OR
Pennsylvania	PA
Puerto Rico	PR
Rhode Island	RI
South Carolina	SC
South Dakota	SD
Tennessee	TN
Texas	TX
Utah	UT
Vermont	VT
Virginia	VA
Virgin Islands	VI
Washington	WA
West Virginia	WV
Wisconsin	WI
Wyoming	WY

4. Publisher's name: When citing a publisher, give the name of the publisher in a brief and clear form. Spell out the names of associations and university presses.

American Psychological Association
The Modern Language Association of America
Harvard Law Review Association of America
Life Insurance Marketing and Research Association
American Library Association
Cambridge University Press

Cornell University Press
Oxford University Press
Princeton University Press
Presses Universitaires de France
University of Chicago Press
University Microfilms International

Omit terms such as *Publishers, Co.,* or *Inc.* that are not needed to easily identify the publisher:

Harcourt Brace Javanovich
Avon Books
Mitchell Press
Government Printing Office
Macmillan
South-Western
Viking Press
Wiley

Application Activities

For each of the sources listed below write a bibliographic citation and a parenthetical note in both the MLA style and the APA style. Use the examples represented in this chapter as your guide.

1. The source is an article by Julie Liesse Erickson entitled "Picking Panel Members to Pass Judgment" which appeared in the February 13, 1986, edition of *Advertising Age*. The article begins on page 12 and continues on page 16. Your reference is to material on page 12.

2. The source is an anthology entitled *Global Macroeconomic Perspectives*, edited by Jagdish N. Sheth and Abdolreza Eshghi, with a 1990 copyright date. The publisher is South-Western Publishing Company in Cincinnati, Ohio. Your reference is to material on page 15.

3. The source is a book by Edith Gilson with Susan Kane. The title is *Unnecessary Choices: The Hidden Life of the Executive Woman*. It was published in New York by William Morrow with a copyright date of 1987. Your reference is to material on pages 66-75.

4. The source is a book by Alvin Toffler entitled *The Adaptive Corporation*, published in New York by McGraw-Hill, Inc., in 1985. Your reference is to material from pages 82-95. In your paper you are also using material from Alvin Toffler's *The Culture Consumers: A Study of Art and Affluence in America*, published by St. Martin's Press, Inc., in 1964 in New York.

5. The source is a video casstte recording entitled *In Search of Excellence*, by Thomas J. Peters and Robert H. Waterman. It was produced by Nathan Tyler Productions in 1985 in Waltham, Massachusetts.

6. The source is an article entitled "Trade Deficit: Worst May Well Be Over," by Craig Stock which appeared in the December 1, 1985, edition of *The Philadelphia Inquirer* on page 1 of section C.
7. The source is an article entitled "Relationships of the Dimension of Intercultural Communication Competence" by Guo-Ming Chen which appeared in the journal *Communication Quarterly*, volume 37, published in 1989. Your reference is to information on pages 118-131.
8. The source is a book by Benjamin B. Tregoe, John W. Zimmerman, Ronald A. Smith, and Peter M. Tobia entitled *Vision in Action: Putting a Winning Strategy to Work.* The book was published in New York in 1989 by Simon and Schuster. Your reference is to information on pages 166-170.
9. The source is an unsigned article entitled "Gains by Light Trucks Cushion Car Sales' Fall," which appeared in the *Chicago Tribune* on January 5, 1990. Your reference is to material in section 3, page 1.
10. The source is a book by Robert D. Reid entitled *Hospitality Marketing Management.* It is a second edition published in New York in 1989 by Van Nostrand Reinhold. Your reference is to information on pages 227-232.

10
FINALIZING
THE BUSINESS
RESEARCH PAPER

LEARNING OBJECTIVE: Upon completing this chapter you should be able to:

1. Assemble the sections of the paper into a correct format that is ready for submission to your instructor.

10.1 General Preparation Guidelines

You want the final copy of your business research paper to reflect the effort you have put into its completion. To ensure a professional appearance, follow the general guidelines below. In addition, determine whether your instructor has additional particular requirements.

1. Use a high-quality printer with standard typeface and a new ribbon. Print your paper on white, 8½″ × 11″ bond typing paper.

2. Use 1″ margins at the top, the bottom, and on the left side of the page. Avoid dividing words at the end of a line. Instead, leave the line short and begin the word on the next line. Word-processing programs with "automatic word-wrap" will move the whole word from the right margin to begin the next line.

3. Make sure your pages are in correct order. Number each page in the upper right hand corner without abbreviation "p." Place the page number one inch from the right edge of the paper and a half-inch from the top. On each page place your last name next to the page number. If the pages of your paper are lost or misplaced, it will be easier for your instructor to keep track of the individual papers.

4. Your paper will be subdivided into a number of basic parts, depending on the documentation style you are using and other spe-

cial requirements of your instructor. Those parts will include all or some of the following:

1. Title page
2. Outline
3. Abstract
4. Text of paper
5. Supplementary notes (if any)
6. Appendix
7. List of sources

10.2 ASSEMBLING PARTS OF THE BUSINESS RESEARCH PAPER

TITLE PAGE

Although MLA style does not recommend a separate title page or an outline page, many instructors require both. If you do not need a separate title page, in the upper left hand column of your first page place your name in full, the professor's name, the title of the course, and the date. If you do need a separate title page, center the title and include all identifying information. The title of the paper should not be enclosed in quotation marks or underlined. Lines should be double-spaced and balanced as shown on the facing page:

STARTING A SUCCESSFUL CATERING BUSINESS

BY

LYNNE REICHMAN

ENGLISH COMPOSITION #404

PROFESSOR MARY SMITH

MAY 4, 1992

OUTLINE

If an outline is required, it should follow the title page. For a discussion of outlining see 8.2.2, "Constructing an Outline."

ABSTRACT

An abstract is a brief summary (75–125 words) of the major points that you make in your paper. To minimize possible confusion, place the abstract on a separate page between the title page (or outline) and the first page of your text. Include your conclusions and make your writing clear and specific.

```
                Starting a Successful Catering Business


        This paper provides a general discussion of the

   necessary steps involved in beginning a catering

   business.  Starting with prerequisites, the study

   focuses on marketing research, product mix,

   marketing and advertising, financial and legal

   matters, pricing, packaging, and budgeting. The

   study concludes that catering can be an enjoyable

   and profitable business venture.
```

TEXT OF PAPER

The introduction, the body, and the conclusion are the three major parts of the text (See chapter 7). Avoid using headings or subtitles to develop your thesis. Instead use continuous paragraphing from one page to the next. The closing page of the text should end with the conclusion of your research. Begin the works cited or references on a new page.

SUPPLEMENTARY NOTES

You may wish to include some supplementary notes which would not comfortably fit into an in-text notation. Place supplementary notes on a separate page after the last paragraph of your text. Label this page *Notes* and center it one inch from the top of the page. In the text of your paper, place the superscript numeral one half space above the line. Include the complete documentation of supplementary notes in the works cited.

APPENDIX

Place supplementary material in the appendix preceding the list of sources. The appendix is a suitable location for charts, tables, figures, and questionnaire results. If you have more than one supplementary item, begin each on a separate page and label as *Appendix A, Appendix B,* and so forth.

LIST OF SOURCES

Centered, and one inch from the top of the paper, label the page *Works Cited* or *References*. Double-space all entries and double-space between the entries.

10.3 SAMPLE BUSINESS RESEARCH PAPERS

The two sample business research papers that follow are included to provide examples of both MLA and APA documentation styles. Both papers are primarily analytical/persuasive in purpose in that they present a point of view or thesis which is then supported by evidence. Such papers differ from informational reports which simply summarize the research on a particular subject. The examples shown are intended to be examples of student writing.

MLA—Sample Title,
Thesis, and Outline Page.

Lynne Reichman

Professor Smith

English Composition #404

4 May 1992

Starting A Successful Catering Business

THESIS: A combination of dedication, proper

            market research and a thorough

            knowledge of the food and beverage

            business will ensure the success of

            your new catering business.

  I.   Introduction

 II.   Characteristics of a Caterer

        A. Evaluating your qualifications.

        B. Determining your financial position.

        C. Making the time commitment.

III.   Preliminary Market Research

MLA style does not require a separate title, thesis, and outline page. If your instructor requires a title, thesis, and outline page, follow this format. If not, follow the format on page 199.

Reichman 2

      A. Analyzing the community.

      B. Analyzing the catering potential.

IV. Deciding What Services to Offer

      A. On-Premises catering.

      B. Off-Premises catering.

       C. In-Home catering.

   V. Marketing Your Business

      A. What is marketing?

       B. Basics

      C. Creating a market.

      D. Effective advertising.

  VI. Learning Financial and Legal

       Considerations

      A. Hiring a lawyer.

      B. Hiring an accountant.

 VII. Setting a Price

      A. Determining food cost percent.

      B. Determining labor cost.

      C. Determining operating costs.

Reichman 3

          D. Deciding desired profit.

VIII. Using Package Plans

          A. Increasing sales.

          B. Attracting customers.

  IX. Budgeting and the Shakedown Period

   X. Conclusion

> **Place the author's last name and page number (1) in the upper right-hand corner. Number all subsequent pages in the same manner.**

> **MLA—First page of paper with title.**

Reichman 1

Lynne Reichman

Professor Smith

Composition 404

4 May 1992

> **Place the title on the first page centered and correctly capitalized.**

Starting A Successful Catering Business

Have you ever had dreams of hosting a magnificent party where the women wear fancy dresses and the men are in black tie, the food is exquisite and the decorations transform the room into a fairyland? Or maybe Have you ever had dreams of having an evening beach party and clambake at your oceanfront house? But, your dreams are not to invite your friend to your beachfront house, and you do not have any friends who would really feel comfortable in a tuxedo; instead you would rather be the one who successfully organizes and executes the function. This love of cooking in combination with

> **Use 1-inch margins at the sides, top, and bottom of all pages.**

> **Do not hyphenate words at the right-hand margins.**

In her own words, the author presents a scenario to introduce her thesis.

Reichman 2

good interpersonal skills could create the base for a successful catering career. There is undoubtably much more to catering than a love of cooking or of making people happy. A combination of dedication, proper market research and a thorough knowledge of the food and beverage business will ensure the success of your catering business.

You have decided to start a catering business. Before going out and buying a building and all the equipment, you should evaluate your qualifications because a love of cooking will not pay the bills. First and formost, you need at least a basic knowledge of food. You should also be familiar with service rules and the various types of food service. An aesthetic ability such as ice carving or cake decorating is a good seller and can be a big asset in your business. You should also be a good mixer and possess the ability to deal with all types of people, both your clients and your employees.

Reichman 3

Another important consideration is your financial position. Will you be able to afford the initial outlay of money for equipment and a building and renovations? Will you be able to get a loan for the money? Catering can take an enormous outlay of money to get started and it may be hard to pay off loans at the start when business is slow. This must be considered also. The question of your time commitment is last. Is this going to be a full-time job or just part-time? If you choose part-time, will you be able to pay your bills? Many caterers work part-time from their houses just to supplement a spouse's income and then become full-time once established. You must consider all of these characteristics and commitments before making your decision.

There is yet another step to research before deciding to open your own catering business. This perhaps is the most important.

Reichman 4

It is preliminary market research which will tell
you whether your business will fail or succeed. You
can use telephone or mail surveys and send them, not
to people in the community, but instead to church,
temple, and synagogue offices,and also social
organizations asking them about functions they hold
throughout the year. Ask them if they rent out
their kitchen facilities. Therefore, you can
benefit two ways: you can cater their functions and
use their banquet halls for independent functions.

    There are several distinct types of caterers
which include: on-premises and off-premises
catering, and in-home cooking. Characteristics of
on-premise catering include the cooking and serving
of meals all in the same hall. It requires the
biggest initial investment (building, commissary,
tables, chairs, linens, silver and crystal). You
need to have the Board of Health inspectors come in
and also the fire department. Off-premises

Reichman 5

catering is the way most caterers get their start.
Cooking is done partially or entirely in your base
kitchen then transported to the location of the
function. You can either renovate your home kitchen
to fit fire and safety regulations or buy a building
with a kitchen. Both will have to have Board of
Health inspections. The initial investment is still
quite high. The easiest way to start a catering
business is an accommodator service. The only
investment you need to make is in a good set
of knives and some chef whites. All the cooking and
serving is done entirely in the client's home
(Splaver 6-7). No inspections are needed in this
type of catering.

Once you have decided that you can make a
catering business succeed and you have decided what
type of services to offer, you need to begin
marketing. First one needs to understand what
marketing is. Marketing is anything that helps

Definition of
marketing as it relates
to the catering business.

Reichman 6

capture a customer's attention, breaks down sales
resistance and gives the customer the slightest
additional reason to notice you and become
interested in what you have to offer (Holtz 34).   If
you do marketing correctly, your business will grow
and you will make money. If you do marketing
incorrectly, your business will flounder (Ketterer
1). The basics of marketing include knowing
what you will sell, to whom you will sell and how
you will reach those to whom you propose to sell
(Holtz 59). This is an in- depth marketing study
where you will focus on the people's needs
and desires. Next,you need to do research, talk to
people and ask questions. This is accomplished
through telephone and mail surveys. Creating a
market is another important marketing skill.
The first rule is to be patient because success does
not start overnight. Initially, you should offer
your services for upcoming community events free of

Reichman 7

charge or at a nominal rate. To be accepted by the
community, you must make yourself known;
consequently the better you are known the more
successful you will be (Splaver 8). Advertising is
the final step for the caterer to take. The most
common method is newspaper or yellow pages ad, but
there are other methods. You can also actively
search the newspapers for engagement announcements
and reunion listings. Once you find the listings,
send out letters stating your services. Direct
mailing can be slightly expensive, but they are
usually well worth the cost. You must remember that
marketing has to be a continuous function
(Holtz 79).

Hiring a lawyer and an accountant before
opening a business is very important. Both should
have prior restaurant experience. Your accountant
will arrange your sales and tax identification
numbers, set up your operating budget, check your

The parenthetical citation is keyed to the works cited list.

Reichman 8

operating costs, and do your year-end bookkeeping.
Your lawyer will know the laws you are subject to
including zoning, health, and liquor laws. He will
also be able to decide the best insurance for you.
Together they should be able to save you
considerable amounts of money initially.

Perhaps one of the most difficult tasks you
will be faced with is the setting of a price for
each function. Food cost, labor cost, operating
costs, and desired profit will all need to be
considered. Food cost is determined by costing out
standard recipes, conducting yield tests, and
dividing to arrive at a food cost percentage. This
percentage will be added into the cost of the food.
The food cost percentage will remain the same for
all functions but should be checked two to three
times per year or when food prices go up greatly.
Labor cost is figured per function by knowing how
many employees you will need and their wages.

Writer presents difficulties
costs create.

Reichman 9

Benefits also need to be included. Operating costs
include rent, taxes, heat, and advertising. These
are added to each function's bill either as an
overall percentage or a dollar- conversion on a per
person basis. Finally, desired profit is added at
the end of the bill. The profit is whatever your
decide, but it should be within reason. If the
client feels your price is too high, the profit will
have to be lowered to make it a little more
acceptable to the client. Once you arrive at your
prices, compare them to your competition's to see
how you compete. Remember that your prices do not
have to mirror your competitions for you to succeed.

There is a way for you to increase your sales
periodically. That is with the use of an occasional
marketing strategy called package plans. Offering
more than one product or service together to the
consumer for one total price is packaging and it
helps to make products appear more attractive

> **Examples reinforce author's point.**

Reichman 10

(Nykiel 156). The consumer is often more apt to
select the package plan because it aids in the
organization of an affair, and the consumer feels
that he or she is getting something for free. Each
package should also include a notation that
customized packages and plans are available. As a
result, the consumer will feel that the package is
tailor made at a more economical price than that of
the competition. Package plans are designed to
increase sales during the slow season so you, the
caterer, are still making a considerable profit even
though the customer is getting a good
deal.

Your accountant will assist you in making a
budget forecasting your sales and expenses before
opening. But be prepared for many cost patterns to
be markedly different from what you had so carefully
planned. This is called the shakedown period during
which operations, cost patterns, and systems for

The author explains
obstacles created
during shakedown
period.

Reichman 11

performing functions will gradually evolve (Splaver 15). You must remember not to get discouraged. This period can be rough. However, after the first year your budget will be better defined, and all of your operating procedures will be second nature. Remember that the shakedown period is a time to iron out difficulties; therefore do not expect it to be your most successful or best period. This period is perhaps the time when hard work and dedication are most important.

With determination, dedication, and a thorough knowledge of the food and beverage business you can make your catering business successful if you conduct proper market research. You cannot expect this to be easy but with a little research you can learn the best methods of conducting this analysis, and you can also learn the best way to make the market work for you. In many areas, there is an extensive market for caterers who are creative and

In her own words, the author summarizes her strategy for a successful catering business.

Reichman 12

very good. All you have to do is have the knowledge
and incentive to make the market come to you. If
you can accomplish this, you will have many
successful and happy but hardworking years ahead.

Indent five spaces.

Reichman 13

Works Cited

Double-space.

Cohen, William A., and Marshall E. Reddick.

Successful Marketing for Small Business.

New York: AMA, 1981.

Dunsmore, Marcia. Personal interview. 7 April

1990.

Holtz, Herman R. The Secrets of Practical

Marketing for Small Business. Englewood

Cliffs, NJ: Prentice, 1982.

Ketterer, Manfred. How to Manage a Successful

Catering Business. Jenks, OK:

J.Williams, 1987.

Lawrence, Elizabeth. The Complete Caterer. New

York: Doubleday, 1988.

Nykiel, Ronald A. Marketing in the Hospitality

Industry. 2nd ed. New York: Van

Nostrand, 1989.

Splaver, Bernard R. Successful Catering.

Ed. Jule Wilkinson. Boston: CBI, 1975.

Double-space.

APA—sample title page.

Number pages consecutively, beginning with title page.

Identify each page with a short title of the paper. Place title a double space above the page number.

Subliminal Communication

1

Center title on the page. Type title in uppercase and lowercase letters. Do not underline the title.

Subliminal Communication in Advertising

Jennifer Musselman

Johnson and Wales University

Type your name and your school in uppercase and lowercase letters.

APA—Abstract

Place the short title and page number (2) in the upper right-hand corner.

Subliminal Communication

2

Center the word *Abstract*.

Abstract

Persuasive advertising causes change in the particular buying behavior of consumers. Techniques of subliminal communication gained public attention in the 1950's when subliminal messages increased the sale of food products. Research exists on how advertisers use subliminal communication to send out visual or aural messages. These subliminal messages are aimed at the subconscious level of consumers who are unaware that their motivation for buying has been changed.

Type the abstract in full block form.

Double-space the abstract.

APA—Frist page of paper

Place the short title and page number (3) in the upper right-hand corner. Number all subsequent pages in the same manner.

Subliminal Communication

3

Place title on the first page, centered and correctly capitalized.

Subliminal Communication in Advertising

Begin the first paragraph a double space below the title.

The scene is a local shopping mall buzzing with crowds of happy shoppers. The focus is a fashionable clothing store, where a teenage girl is sneaking a pair of Guess jeans into her backpack. Suddenly, she is overwhelmed by an unexplainable impulse to put the hot item back on the rack.   Indent all paragraphs 5 spaces.

In another incident, a young couple is seated in a local movie theater. Suddenly, they are both craving the hot, buttered popcorn and an icy cold Coke. This is unexplainable since they ate not twenty minutes before.

Are these just stories, or is there some reasoning behind the unexplainable actions of the characters? Ask someresearchers and they will tell you it is "coincidental." But ask the store owner,

Double-space text of paper.

Opening paragraphs prepare reader for the thesis.

Use 1½-inch margins at sides, top, and bottom of all pages.

Subliminal Communication

4

the movie theater owner, or other researchers, and you will hear otherwise. In both cases some form of subliminal communication was used. The shoplifter's surge of honesty was inspired by a voice she could not really hear. That is because under the lines of "We Didn't Start The Fire" blasting from the store's speakers, there are the messages: "Be Honest!", Don't Steal!", "We Arrest Shoplifters!". These are digitally being mixed with this Billy Joel hit. The hungry couple's cravings are caused by the messages: "Hungry? Eat Popcorn!", "Drink Coca-Cola!" that are repeatedly flashed on the screen. Unbelievable? Not so. We all have been exposed to some form of subliminal communication, though most of us do not even realize it.

Subliminal communication is based on the idea that we can detect information presented below our threshold of awareness. People exposed to subliminal

Introduction narrows to thesis.

Do not hyphenate words at the right-hand margin.

Thesis is defined.   Subliminal Communication

5

messages flashed on a movie or television screen,
embedded in a magazine ad or audio tape may not
consciously see or hear anything beyond the obvious,
but they are supposed to be aware of the messages at
an unconscious level. Apparently, stimuli enter the
brain where the important bits of information are
referred to the conscious mind for special
attention. The rest it responds to subconsciously
(Lander, 1981).

One may be aware of this presorting, for
example, when someone is talking to you while you
are in a moving car with the windows down or on a
busy street near a construction site. Some words,
though not clearly heard, may cause you to "perk up"
and try to understand.

According to Taylor (1986), subliminal
communication is much older than one might think.
As far back as the turn of the century, the concept
of the subliminal mind was one of controversy.
Subliminal perception first gained public attention

In the text, author is
cited by last name
only.

Underline
words to draw
reader's
attention.

Subliminal Communication

6

Underline movie titles.

in the 1950's when a New Jersey theater owner
reported flashing refreshment subliminals during the
showing of the movie, <u>Picnic</u>. According to claims,
flashing the words "Drink Coca-Cola" and "Eat
popcorn" resulted in a fifty-eight percent
increase in the sale of these products. People
scoffed at the very thought of being tricked into
buying popcorn, and so subliminal persuasion
dwindled in the later fifties and did not
revive again until the seventies.

In the seventies, subliminal messages appeared
almost everywhere. In magazine ads, subliminal
messages showed up as sexual images hidden in
pictures. In horror films, moviemakers
tried to maximize scare potential by flashing death
masks and other frightening images on the screen.
And, for the first time, people "heard" subliminal
messages. To discourage shoplifting, store's buried
"I am honest" messages in their music, and to
increase sales, real estate companies subjected

Combination of direct quotation and paraphrase.

their agents to tapes with hidden motivational
phrases.

　　These days subliminal communication has greatly
increased and expanded to a variety of other uses.
Research indicates that attempts are being made by
the media to manipulate the general public through
the use of subliminals. Some resorts use
subliminals to help vacationers relax. Computer
programs flash subliminal messages during television
shows. And video and audio tapes that offer
subliminal solutions for problems ranging from
excess weight to stress are hot items at stores
everywhere.

　　The formats of tapes are similar to the music
recordings played in stores. Many of them play
soothing music or the sound of waves lapping against
shorelines, while the listener or viewer receives
subliminal messages. On audio tapes, messages
such as "I eat less" and "I am calm" are either
speeded up or played at a very low volume. Either

Short quotations
integrated into the
text .

Information
supports
thesis.

Subliminal Communication

8

way, they can not be deciphered or heard. Videos

flash messages so fast-they last about 1/30th of a

second or less-that the viewer does not consciously

see them (Natale, 1988).

How well these messages work seems to depend on

the person exposed to them. "Some research

indicates that subliminal messages can simulate

basic drives, such as hunger, but they do not appear

to work equally well on everyone, and stimulation

does not necessarily trigger action" (Moore, 1985,

p. 11).

In his book, <u>Subliminal Learning</u>, Taylor

(1988), shows that what is subliminal for one person

may be as plain as day to another. And some people

may respond immediately to a subliminal message,

while others have a delayed response or no response

at all.

The research on subliminals used by advertising

people has been well-documented by W.B. Key, a

communications expert. Key has said that every

Subliminal Communication

9

major advertising agency has at least one "embedding technician" in its art department. Ads frequently use sexual imageries to trigger purchasing behavior. This technique does sell the news which sells the advertising, which sells the product. In his popular book, <u>Subliminal Seduction</u> (1981), Key stated the following:

> Selling products in this country involves big money, and business people want all the leverage they can get for their investment. If there is something to subliminal manipulation (and indeed there is), businessmen want to take advantage of it. (p. 187)

Enough research exists on subliminal perception to establish it as a psychological phenomenon, but psychologists say more is needed, especially with tapes. One psychologist, Shevrin, argues that behavioral change may occur, but it is

Double-space before and after long quotations. Indent five spaces from the left margin. No need for quotations marks.

Subliminal Communication

10

nearly impossible to trace the change to a

subliminal message on tape. In short, Shevrin says

of tapes, "It's a scam. Their catalogues refer to

scientific research but omit specifics. When I

write to ask for the evidence, they don't reply. If

the results were there, wouldn't the tape companies

be the first to cite them" (cited in Natale, 1988,

p. 29)? **Primary source is cited in secondary source.**

However, according to Robert Deckert, Professor

of Psychiatry and Behavioral Sciences at the

University of Oklahoma Health Sciences Center,

subliminal learning tapes do have an effect on

listeners.

> Subliminal messages can shape behavior.
> There's no question about that. The real
> question is not does it work, but how well does
> it work? People who use these tapes will lose
> weight, for example, but whether they'll
> lose the weight and keep it off is no more

Subliminal Communication

11

guaranteed than with other techniques for losing weight. (cited in "Subliminal Learning," 1989, p. 8)

Most people are surprised to learn that there are no laws regulating subliminal communication. There is no protection from subliminal manipulation, except maybe trying to understand it. As a matter of fact, very little has been done to curb this activity. In 1957, when Vance Packard published The Hidden Persuaders, legislation, on the national and state levels, was proposed to control subliminal messages hidden in advertising, but none of the proposed bills have become law. And in 1973 the Federal Communications Commission tried to ban the use of subliminals on television when a commercial for a children's game was claimed to have had the subliminal message "Get it!". But again, nothing has ever passed (Zajonc, 1986)

Subliminal Communication

12

Chances are, this very day, every time you looked at a television commercial, or an ad in print, you were probably being assaulted by, or at least exposed to, devices your conscious mind cannot detect. This may bother you, but then again, maybe it does not. Maybe there are actually people out in the world who do not mind that they really can be tricked into buying a certain product or behaving a certain way, just as long as they are aware of what is going on. As research continues and we learn more about the potential of subliminal communication, the old warning to consumers seems appropriate. "Caveat Emptor"--Let the Buyer Beware.

Concluding paragraph echoes thesis.

Subliminal Communication

13

Double-space all
reference entries.

References

Key, W. B. (1981). <u>Subliminal seduction</u>. Englewood
    Cliffs, NJ: Prentice Hall.

Lander, E. (1981, February). In through the out
    door. <u>Omni</u>, p. 44-49.

Moore, T. E. (1985, July). Subliminal delusion.
    <u>Psychology Today</u>, p. 10-12.

Natale, J. A. (1988, September). Are you open to
    suggestion? <u>Psychology Today</u>, p. 28-29.

Taylor E. (1986). <u>Subliminal communication</u>. Salt
    Lake City: JAR.

Taylor E. (1988). <u>Subliminal learning: An eclectic
    approach</u>. Salt Lake City: JAR.

Subliminal learning: A fraud. (1989, September). <u>USA
    Today</u>, p. 8.

Zajonc, R. B. (1986, February). Mining new gold from
    old research. <u>Psychology Today</u>, p. 51.

Indent three spaces.

Single-space.

Works Cited

Accountants Index. 1988.

America's Most Hospitable Cities Survey. Providence: Johnson & Wales U, 1989.

Brauchli, Marcus, W. "Japanese Investors Try to Quell Fear They'll Ditch U.S. Holdings." *Wall Street Journal* 2 Feb. 1990: C1.

Bryant, Joyce E., Nancy H. Baran, and Sharon M. Tarrant, eds. *Your Guide for Teaching Money Management.* Prospect Heights: Household International, 1988.

Bryant, Web. "Women Entrepreneurs: Who Are They? More Women Mean Business." *USA Today* 21 June 1989: 4B.

Business Periodicals Index. Apr. 1989.

Drucker, Peter, F. *The Frontiers of Management: Where Tomorrow's Decisions are Being Shaped Today.* New York: Talley-Truman, 1986.

Farrell, Thomas, J. *Developing Writing Skills.* Providence: PAR, 1985.

"Federal Express Spreads Its Wings." *Journal of Business Strategy.* July-Aug. 1988: 15-20.

Finlay, Douglas. "Don't Wait Until You Get Burned." *Administrative Management* Mar. 1988: 22.

Gibaldi, Joseph, and Walter S. Achtert, eds. *MLA Handbook for Writers of Research Papers.* 3rd ed. New York: MLA, 1988.

Metzger, Jeff. Letter to Researcher. 12 Aug. 1989.

Miller, Lawrence M. *American Spirit: Visions of a New Corporate Culture.* New York: Morrow, 1984.

Murray, Donald. *A Writer Teaches Writing.* Boston: Houghton, 1984.

New York Times Quaterly Index. Apr.-June 1989.

Public Affairs Information Services Bulletin. Mar. 1989.

Publication Manual of the American Psychological Association. 3rd ed. Washington: APA, 1989.

Reader's Guide to Periodical Literature. 10 Apr. 1989.

Vogel, Shawna. "Disease of the Year: Illness as Glitch." *Discover* Jan., 1989.

Wall Street Journal Index. Mar. 1989.

Warren, Virginia. *Guidelines for Non-Sexist Use of Language.* Newark, DE: U of Delaware, 1990.

Zinsser, William. "Rewriting." *On Writing Well.* New York: Harper, 1980.

Index